Praise for The Song of the Fall

"Astounding in length and depth…the extent of your research and your mastery of these events places your work far above just about every project I have ever seen…the voice of authority—or author-ity—is the hardest achievement for any writer, old or young. You have your voice."

—*Dava Sobel, author of Longitude,*
Galileo's Daughter, and The Planets

"Outstanding both in the sense that it's not something you see every day and in the sense that it's a very accomplished piece of writing…impressively well-versed in the conventions of epic poetry, in the details of the fall of Constantinople, and in the medieval history and antiquity more generally…"

—*John Siciliano, editor, Penguin Classics*

"An imaginative poem! The theme of religious war between Christians and Muslims resonates today…clear and eloquent."

—*David Reynolds, author of John Brown: Abolitionist, Walt*
Whitman's America: a Cultural Biography, and winner of the
Bancroft Prize and the

"The most impressive project in its s‹ have ever seen."

T0204447

—*Dr. Richard M. Dunn, author of Geo*
Circle: Literary and Aesthetic Life in the Early 20ᵗʰ Century

"A tremendous project—thoroughly researched in both historical detail and literary style."

—*Andrew Wylie, president of The Wylie Agency*

THE SONG OF THE FALL

THE SONG OF THE FALL

CHRISTOPHER IMPIGLIA

an epic poem

TATE PUBLISHING & Enterprises

The Song of the Fall
This title is also available as a Tate Out Loud product.
Visit www.tatepublishing.com for more information.
Copyright © 2010 by Christopher Impiglia. All rights reserved.

No part of this publication may be reproduced, stored in a retrieval system or transmitted in any way by any means, electronic, mechanical, photocopy, recording or otherwise without the prior permission of the author except as provided by USA copyright law.

The opinions expressed by the author are not necessarily those of Tate Publishing, LLC.

Published by Tate Publishing & Enterprises, LLC
127 E. Trade Center Terrace | Mustang, Oklahoma 73064 USA
1.888.361.9473 | www.tatepublishing.com

Tate Publishing is committed to excellence in the publishing industry. The company reflects the philosophy established by the founders, based on Psalm 68:11,
"The Lord gave the word and great was the company of those who published it."

Book design copyright © 2010 by Tate Publishing, LLC. All rights reserved.
Cover design by Blake Brasor
Interior design by Joel Uber
Cover art by Giancarlo Impiglia

Published in the United States of America

ISBN: 978-1-61663-991-4
1. Poetry / Epic
2. History / Medieval
10.09.13

Table of Contents

The Definition of an Epic Poem 9

Note on the Text 11

List of Characters 13

A Saint's Memory 17

When a Goth Did Sit in Caesar's Chair 19

The First Encounter of Mohammed and the Romans 23

Heaven's City on Earth 25

The Unfortunate Rise of the Antichrist 29

The Emperor's Throat Is Cut 35

Send Aid, Franks, Lest the Great City Fall 41

Those Who Came to Constantine's Side 45

The Bees Spill from the Hive 49

The Crumbling Stones and the Dragon's Breath 53

The Swift-Footed Before the Wall 57

May the Sea Swallow Mehmet's Slaves 61

Aid from Heaven 65

Hold Fast, Romans, the Pagan's Fury 69

Great Constantine, What Courage Lays in Your Heart! 75

The Failing Faith   79
Romans, Look Upon the Apocalypse, and Be Brave!   85
Constantine's Stand   93
What Becomes of Us   99
Final Historical Note   103
Suggested Reading List   107
Notes   111

The Definition of an Epic Poem

What makes this poem epic? According to the Greeks, any long poem written in dactylic hexameter was considered an epic. This definition changed, however, to include any narrative poem with a theme based around the gods, heroes, war, and adventure. Poems such as the Iliad, the father of all epics, were originally oral in nature and were memorized and then performed by a bard at a court or any circle of high society. The Iliad presented readers and listeners with eternal messages on social life, death, immortality, and the effect of time on the individual.

During the Roman period and beyond, epic poems began to take on a didactic role, teaching people how to interact with the gods, and with each other. Knowledge of the Iliad soon became the mark of an educated person, participating, along with the Bible, in the flourishing of Western culture.

The Middle Ages and the Renaissance both witnessed the creation of epics in the image of the Iliad, all intending to do honor to the characters they presented and attempting to be worthy in the eyes of the ancient masterpiece. It is for this very reason that the Iliad was continually reproduced and survives to this day. It continues to be compelling and continues to inspire modern thinkers.

I carry on the legacy of the Iliad, which has inspired authors for thousands of years and has allowed me to sing The Song of the Fall.

Note on the Text

When first approaching the text, it was a difficult decision on what meter to use. If I was to opt to use a historical meter, my choices were endless, from the dactylic hexameter of Homer to the terza rima of Dante. Being a modern epic, however, I felt to simply emulate one of the various styles of a past poem would not be satisfactory. I therefore decided to create a free-verse style of my own, incorporating various stylistic elements of past epics such as the use of alliterative verse in Beowulf. It is a free-flowing style placing emphasis on various parts of the sentence as if it was being orated dramatically, the way in which most epic poems were conveyed long before they were written down. The poem is thus designed so that it should be read aloud for the greatest dramatic effect.

I would like to express that this manuscript does not intend to insult the believers of any religion, nor does it reflect my own religious beliefs. Instead, it is designed to emulate epic poems and medieval manuscripts from a Christian perspective.

List of Characters

in order of appearance

Theodosian II: *The Byzantine emperor from ad 408–450 who constructed the nearly impregnable wall that surrounded Constantinople.*

Constantine XI Palaeologus: *Emperor of Byzantium from ad 1448–14(?).*

Mehmet II: *Sultan of the Ottoman Turks from ad 1444–1446 and 1451–1481.*

Heraclius: *Emperor of Byzantium from ad 610–641.*

Mohammed the Messenger: *The Prophet of Allah as described in the Koran.*

Murat: *The sultan predecessor to Mehmet II.*

Ahmet: *Sultan Murat's son.*

George Sphrantzes: *A good friend of Emperor Constantine XI and ambassador of the Byzantine Empire.*

Muhrad: *The father of Mehmet II.*

Gabriel: *Herald of God as described in the Bible.*

Antonio Rizzo: *The Venetian captain of a trading vessel with duties in the Black Sea.*

Giovanni Giustiniani Longo: *A lord from Genoa who came to the aid of the Byzantines at his own expense.*

Troilo, Paolo, and Antonio Bocchiardo: *Genoese brothers from a wealthy family who came to the aid of the Byzantines at their own expense.*

Don Francisco of Toledo: *A Castilian noble who went to Constantinople and befriended the emperor.*

John Grant of Germany: *Unlike his name suggests, he was a Scottish engineer who, like Don Francisco, came to Constantinople and befriended the emperor.*

Karaja Pasha: *An Ottoman noble who converted to Islam after being raised as a Christian.*

Ishak Pasha: *An Ottoman noble who led the Anatolian section of the Ottoman army.*

Mahmut Pasha: *An Ottoman noble who, with Ishak Pasha, led the Anatolian section of the Ottoman army.*

Nicephorus Palaeologus: *A relative of Constantine XI.*

Loukas Notaras: *The Grand Duke of Constantinople.*

Demetrios Palaeologus: *The younger brother of Constantine XI.*

Theophilus Palaeologus: *A relative of Constantine XI who traveled extensively in Europe and was very learned in the ways of chivalry.*

Theodore of Karystes: *An elderly, learned scholar and noble of the Byzantine Empire.*

Baltaoglu: *The commander of the Ottoman navy.*

Zorzi Doria: *A great lord of Genoa who came to the aid of the Byzantines.*

Giacomo Coco: *A Venetian naval commander.*

Murat the Janissary: *The leader of the unit of Ottoman troops known as the Janissaries.*

Omar Bey: *The standard bearer of the Ottoman army.*

A Saint's Memory

Hwaet![1] That may Lord Jesus Christ in his mercy
place upon me righteous measure,
and in His name,
and in the name of his most holy mother Mary—
upon whose bosom He lay
in a moment of darkness,
after from the cross He was pulled down for the sins of us mortals—
may I sing of greatness.
And beneath this most holy influence,
let the saints rain down their memories
that I may tell of the horror correctly,
for the mortal mind may wither
even if it was entrusted
with the greatest of memories.
For not only have I witnessed the event,
the Saints and God himself looked on
in sorrow and in mourning.
I invoke the minds of the most holy,
lest I should not give proper praise

to those who deserve it most.[2]
The rape of Constantinople burned deep
in the heart of all us Christian brothers,
for although our differences threatened to cast us apart,
in the heat of battle
did it bring us together, and in holy light did we shine,
steadfast in the eye of the pagan.
Orthodox and Catholic, even the pagan in his hovel,
brought together
in a struggle worthy of David.
The walls of heaven shuddered
when the walls of Theodosian[3] crumbled.
Brave Romans! Strong-hearted sons of Romulus![4]
Constantine Palaeologus,
in Christ true Emperor and Autocrat of the Romans,
and vile Mehmet, who would see his downfall.
It would be the fall of glory,
the fall of reason, the fall of righteousness,
but in it all would God bring us new glory, new reason
that we may flourish again,
and in a renewed righteousness would we live.
The Christians who perished gave us new life.
He who survived
passed on what could have been lost forever.
Constantinople,
the highest glory of the Christian world,
would fall to the pagans,
but its greatest moment
would never die.
For I shall tell of it,
and it will always last.[5]

When a Goth Did Sit
in Caesar's Chair

In the city of Jerusalem, Mohammed the Messenger
confronted the great Heraclius with bold words:
"Undo yourself, wretched unbeliever.
In the name of the Faith, Allah,
the most benevolent.
Peace be upon those who embrace Him
and surrender to His graces.
Embrace the Faith and
Allah will bestow on you a double reward.
Embrace it not, and in your wrong doings
will your people suffer
under your misguided rule."[6]
It had begun when the West had fallen,
a Goth now sat on Rome's throne.
The true God had not been embraced in the West,
and God saw it fit
that the Romans should no longer wield power.

The East, embracing the true faith,
was graced by His holy measures,
which in His name flourished, and built for Him Saint Sophia,
a house of worship
unrivaled in the world.
Heraclius, son of Heraclius, ruled at this time.
Strong was his presence.
He alone brought down the vile Sassanids,
and in God's name
did he give rise to a new and stronger empire.[7]
It was he who recovered the lost remnants of wood
that our Lord Jesus Christ himself
was nailed upon.
Deep in the East, the wood was hidden,
rotting under Persian feet,
until Heraclius came.
Strong-armed Heraclius the wise, the learned, with his vast army
marched beneath His gaze and in His name
reclaimed what was lost.
He restored the sacred wood in his great city,
and there it would still lie
amongst the beams of light that
did shine through from heaven,
had the sons of Orhan[8]
never been placed upon this earth.
Lo! Imagine the city restored!
But Heraclius knew none of this.
His faith had led him to Jerusalem to visit the holy city
where Jesus had been placed upon the cross
by those whom he posed a threat to.
His pilgrimage would be disturbed
by a most unholy presence:
The Messenger himself
sought the destruction of mighty God
and the death of those who upheld His name.

Heraclius, the most wise, in his righteousness beneath
the hill where Jesus was crucified,
turned to the one called Mohammed and placed Roman steel
against the pagan's throat.
For who could be so foolish
as to confront one so lofty as Heraclius?
What slave would dare challenge a king
on his holy trek to Jerusalem?
What peasant would confront the great Heraclius,
he who had done so many great deeds
in the name of his empire
and in the name of God?
This was Heraclius, who saw the end of the Sassanids and Slavs!
This was Heraclius, who returned the true cross to Christian lands!
Heraclius sent reply unto this challenger,
who did speak so rudely to such a king.
For only pagan teachings
would allow such a challenge
from one so low to one so great:
"Speak not to me, foul man.
He who calls himself Mohammed, listen well:
My journey to Jerusalem on foot
displays where my allegiance lies.
With God, Lord Jesus, and his mother Mary, do I rule.
Without them would I have become conqueror of vile Sassanids,
who upon their chariots
rode down Christians?
Without them would I have become conqueror of these Persians,
who plagued our lands with bronze and iron?
Without them would I have defeated their kings
who brought to battle beasts of great stature?[9]
Nay, heathen. Bother me not with your wretched babble.
Your words are empty
and under false inspiration.
My religion and my sovereignty will reach limits that

no other kingdom has surpassed."
Mohammed did not flinch at the Roman steel that did point at his throat.
Instead he took a step closer to the great Heraclius
so that the point of the blade
drew a droplet of pagan blood.
And then the Saracen spoke:
"You have decided not to embrace Allah the most benevolent,
and you have decided to be cruel to your people
by doing so.
For in the coming years you will now know only fear,
and Allah will not rest
until you have suffered the greatest evils
for forsaking the true faith."[10]
Heraclius did shudder at these words
but would not dare succumb
to the pagan's resolve.

The First Encounter of Mohammed and the Romans

Not fifty summers passed before the sons of Mohammed
confronted the sons of Heraclius.
Before the Golden Gate of Constantinople
the first blows were struck.
At the walls, fire cast from the sons of Constantine
spread against nature.
When water was placed upon the flames, they only spread,
and in divine light did they feed off pagan souls
and spread amongst the enemy.
The sons of Constantine call it "Fire of the Greeks;"
I call it "Gabriel's Flame,"
and in a fury did it devastate its enemies.[11]
The battle was fierce, and their god, called Allah, failed them,
and we triumphed.
It was here that the grudge formed.
The pagan slaves in their nature are fierce and bloodthirsty.
Defeat they do not take well.

They had tasted
the metal of the Romans, they had tasted
the wrath of the Holy God, and they had tasted
defeat and the betrayal of their God.
But pagan thirst for conquest only grew stronger:
Like a beast being trained for domestic uses, offering it
a piece of flesh and then having it whipped,
so that it may learn
to not be tempted by flesh.
The more the beast is whipped,
the more courageous it learns to become.
It will test the keeper, and its own ability to withstand pain,
before it is again beaten back.
The more we beat the heathens back,
the more courage they obtained.
And they would return to the walls of Theodosian many times.
Constantine's city became the object of their obsession and fury,
and they would return, their fury never quenched,
the words of the slave Mohammed in their hearts.

Heaven's City on Earth

In the year of our Lord 1451,
the beast would return to test the will
of Lord Jesus Christ and the sons of Constantine,
who found a godless world outside their gates.
Sons of Constantine, sons of Romulus!
Sons of mighty God and Mother Mary!
Find courage in your hearts lest the enemy overtake you!
For it was in this year that a changed world was clear.
Constantine's city had become the severed head
of her once great Empire.
Only inside Theodosian's walls was the empire still preserved.
Outside the walls, past the small Roman towns,
a godless world loomed.
To the north, east, and west, the heathen Turks now held sovereignty,
surrounding the city.
The vast lands of the Christian Empire were now no more,
the Turks now dwelling amongst the
blackened ruins that once shined bright in Roman hands.
The heathens had brought a new menace to the land.

Outside the walls only fear lingered.
The city of Constantine was
now a mere skeleton of her former self,
the bones left after the feast of the sad year 1204,
when the Franks[12] did storm the city
and peeled from the walls
great edifices of Constantine's struggle,
the great splendor of ancient Rome,
and relics of the most holy.
The skeleton chattered in the cold brought by the Turks,
who deemed to break into the jail of sanctuary
formed by the bones that surrounded the Romans.
The skeleton, however, remained unrivaled in beauty
in the whole of the East and West.
From the steppes of Asia to the forests of the Franks,
no city shone so bright as Constantinople,
which, like a light illuminated from heaven,
stood amongst a surrounding, darkening cloud.
What splendor there did lay, a time now past!
To look with the eye would be as if to look on heaven,
the blinding, beautiful light
casting the traveler into a divine state.
He would find himself without words;
his eyelids would be unable to shut,
so beautiful was the city.
But beyond the fosse, the fires of hell
stirred and burned away
the remains of Constantine's great struggle.
Beyond the fosse, the pagans scurried to and fro,
picking off with filed teeth the last remains of flesh
from the bones of the skeleton.
Past the Golden Gate,
the gold long since torn off by the Franks,
the emperors of old once passed triumphantly
from a glorious campaign,

bringing with them the lost relics of saints and of The Lord Jesus Christ,
which had been scattered amongst the hills of heathen lands;
Past the Church of Holy Apostles
where inside lay the head of John the Baptist;
Past the Church of Christ,
where the crown of thorns, which rested upon His head,
inside did lay;
Past the great Roman Hippodrome,
the stone benches of which now crumble: its eyes
had seen the great days of the city,
when charioteers did race upon its tracks
and spectators did fill the air with a heavenly din;
Past the lofty image of Justinian atop his horse,
the cross-crested globe clutched in one hand—
with which he did wield power—
for it was without sword or shield that he ruled,
but with the Word of God did he grace the lands;
Past the Church of Saint Irene,
where the nails from the cross are kept,
there did lay the true splendor of the city:
Saint Sophia,[13] where God dwells among men.
There it is said even a whisper can be heard by Him,
and even the most lowly of worshippers
can be granted penance.
For it is in Saint Sophia that
the earth and heaven no longer are a part
of different realms.
There, amongst the glittering marble,
gold-plated ceiling, jewel-encrusted walls,
heaven and earth meet.
Saint Sophia: the kiss of two realms.
Who can describe such beauty?
The sun's rays send golden light,
which splashes across the many colored marbles and
columns reaching to heaven.

Like a spring torrent of rain it falls across the marbled floor,
flooding the vaulted chamber with a golden mist
so bright, so brilliant, worshippers can hardly bear to look![14]
Through such brilliance, our Lord gazes from above
against a dome resembling heaven
He watches down upon us.
Never can we escape His gaze,
and under his gaze did we find comfort,
even with heathens at the gates.
Even with the Turks at the gates—
the pagans who beyond the walls lived in hellish flames
and sought only destruction—
did the Romans hold their faith intact.
Even with the Turks at the gates—
plotting to consume the last of
the great world that once was—
the Romans were safe beneath His watchful eyes.

The Unfortunate Rise of the Antichrist

The year of our Lord 1451 would give rise
to this antichrist on earth.
Mehmet, the Shadow of God,
would ascend to power.
His true character would be revealed in his first days of ascent.
Murat, predecessor of Mehmet, evil in his own right,
was struck down by mighty God,
and none knew it possible
one more hateful than Murat could be born,
since it was Murat who also dared confront the gates of Theodosian,
and did he fail under God's watchful eyes.
Born from hatred did Mehmet arise,
and in his first years did he see it fit
to quench his thirst for blood.
Not even for his own kin did he have compassion—
compassion, a word unknown to such a man,
if he could be called so,

who did kill his kin Ahmet[15]
to secure the throne.
Sorrowful Ahmet!
If only had he grown to confront such a shadow,
Turkish power may not have been
in the hands of such a tyrant as Mehmet,
and only under such a culture as that of Orhan
could such a practice
be considered noble.
Mehmet sent his minion to the chamber of Ahmet,
where the child did bathe,
and the minion submerged the young Ahmet
until life no longer stirred in the child.
Mehmet, following the death of his kin,
was arrogant and foolish and corrupt,
and in the following spring built for himself
a new place of worship,
where their god might be revered.
His foolishness spoke to the Romans when he built this temple
on the soil to the west of Constantine's city:
Roman soil.
With the death of Murat and the construction of the temple,
brave friend of Constantine,
the resourceful George Sphrantzes,
who to the Turks was merely
one to know every manner of shiftiness and crafty counsels,
but, forsooth, was equal to God in counsel,
had done excellent things by thousands,
brought forward good counsel to the emperor.[16]
Sphrantzes, ambassador of the empire, was sent to Edirne[17]
to confront Mehmet.
There, in the chamber of the sultan, George Sphrantzes
placed gifts at the feet of Mehmet,
with gold-spun shoes, and spoke:
"Mehmet, son of Muhrad, from Constantine I bring tidings.

You who have succeeded to the throne of Murat,
I hope you continue to uphold the treaty signed
between your predecessor and my master.
Peace can continue to be had,
if you are wise like the king before you.
Let the treaty stand intact, and keep your people off Roman soil.
You are not permitted to build on the soil of our Lord God
without permission from his highness Constantine,
who, in his mighty presence, does grace you good tidings
if you are to uphold our agreement.
The emperor grieves, however, to hear of the death of young Ahmet,
whose mother was a great friend of my king
and did spend ample time in his city.
Constantine finds it difficult to trust one
who does kill a brother with a noble will."
Mehmet did speak on this matter,
when confronted by George Sphrantzes:
"When ascent is evident, it behooves he who ascends
to kill his brother in the interest of world order.
No order is possible when two brothers seek an identical goal,
for in their plight will they ruin each other,
and their realm beneath them,
in their struggle for the throne.
The jurists of the empire have approved of fratricide,
let action be taken accordingly."[18]
George Sphrantzes shuddered at such barbarous nature
and questioned the sultan:
"My master would embrace you as a brother, should you see fit
that our two empires live in peace,
but it seems that fratricide is a noble deed at your court,
and hence he finds it hard to believe that he who values fratricide
could return a brotherly embrace."
Mehmet, who had been seated in a throne of jewels in a relaxed manner,
stood up, rigid and with a strong gaze.
His hellish splendor was quickly clear,

and silence filled the room when he stood,
as if all felt his fury and silenced themselves in the fear
that emanated from the sultan's breast.
His mail of a thousand scales glinted with a thousand flames,
and his gaze made even one so noble as George Sphranztes
bow under such terrible animation.
The pagan spoke: "And what would you or your master, nonbelievers,
know on the matter of good rule
or the love of one's brother?"
George twittered but did not speak,
as not to anger the pagan any further.
The sultan seated himself once more and continued,
"On the matter of the treaty:
It will be kept on our part so long as Omnipotent Allah sees fit.
Allah, who is most forgiving,
punish us if we should break our vow."
George did bring these words to Constantine:
"Your highness, he did swear upon their most unholy god
and pray that their god
does bind them to their word."
Constantine looked on this matter honestly:
"Let us hope that like our God,
who sees all and watches over us,
to whom we may bind our word,
may their god bind theirs."
"I have seen their court. I have seen their master who they call Mehmet.
And although these Saracens[19] may be barbarous in their very nature,
I too believe
they can hold their word."
Wise beyond all measure, resourceful, mighty Sphrantzes was.
But neither he nor great Constantine could see
that to put trust in a vile being like
Mehmet, who knew not what the word *vow* meant,
and whose pagan beliefs could not bind a word if it came
from the mightiest of men,

CHRISTOPHER IMPIGLIA

would result in the further destruction of the empire.
Constantine, who held such great esteem among men,
and walked among God,
as God's regent on earth,
was foolish to trust the word of this infidel,
who is treacherous in his very nature.
These vile pagans could not be trusted,
and had only the great men of Constantinople noticed this,
the great city might not now lie in ruins.
The Romans had misread the character of the sultan
who upheld his master Mohammed's desire for conquest.

The Emperor's Throat Is Cut

The emperor walked across his great walls,
wise Sphrantzes at his side.
"Look, good George.
Look at what has become of my kingdom.
No longer can I look at the horizon,
and see the empire stretch past it.
To the end of my vision, I now see the fires of unholy camps:
the heathens who now surround our lands.
My dear friend, I have done what I could to bring the land of my father
and his father before him
to its previous splendor.
But it seems we can never recover the loss we suffered
through the betrayal of the wretched Catholics
so many years ago.
I am in desperate need of funds and without the land required
to quench this need."
Sphrantzes spoke to his king: "Do not grieve, my king.
Our walls will never be breached
so long as God is on our side.
So have faith in Him, and leave your fate to Him,

who is the only one
who can weave our future.[20]
He has set down the laws, and He has chosen the lives
of the sons of men.[21]
But I remember the stories told
of a time before the Catholics came.
The brilliant white and red of our walls,
which now are faded after Catholic and Saracen blood
washed against them.
The jeweled statues of your fathers,
who stood guard at the gate,
paneled in gold the wood once was.
There your fathers did march into the city, in full splendor,
decorated with emblems of the conquered peoples.
And they were proud men."
So wise Sphrantzes was, even greater men such as Constantine
heeded his counsel.[22]
If they were to sit next to each other,
Constantine on a throne and George on a wooden stool,
George may yet have been loftier.
"If only I ruled in that time," was Constantine's reply.
George spoke, "If only we both shared a moment in that time."
Constantine could no longer bear the memory of his great city,
when it held its full splendor.
He surveyed his city, a shadow of his former self, and wept.
Tears did stream down his noble face;
into his hoary-white[23] beard they flowed.
God in his lofty seat looked down upon brave Constantine.
He sat wrapped in the misty clouds that swarmed his body;
like a robe they concealed his nakedness.
Just as the tear fell down the face of Constantine,
a tear too passed down the Lord's cheek
and spilled into His beard made of white clouds.
Between the starry sphere and the surface of the earth,
He looked upon the world.
In one glance He looked into the heart of all beings

CHRISTOPHER IMPIGLIA

and saw deep into their desires.
None could escape His gaze, which could see all creatures.
Into the heart of Constantine
He looked and saw only goodness,
only a longing to make right the horrors that were to come,
only a desire to return to the time when the world was good
and the Romans were strong.
He saw George Sphrantzes,
who wanted but to please the emperor and continue
to embrace the emperor in friendship.
He saw Mehmet, and he saw a shadow,
one bent solely on the destruction of
a city constructed in His name
and the ravaging of His holy lands.
He saw Mehmet's wretched plans to destroy the empire,
and grieved for Constantine.
What pity God did feel for the Christians.[24]
And so God called upon Gabriel,
words as pure as Scripture spilled from His lips:
"Go, my great herald,
my messenger to the earth, faithful and great you are.
Find Constantine, and in my name ask,
'Do you not see on the horizon
what the pagan has done?
Look toward the strait that does lead to the Black Sea.
Act quickly, lord who acts on earth, in my stead.
For the great pagan Mehmet
has cut your throat.'"
Gabriel dispatched from the realm of heaven.
Parting the clouds, he let the light from God's realm rain on the earth,
and for a moment the hills of Constantine's empire
were illuminated by the divine light.
Gabriel, messenger of the Lord, herald of God, departed with all haste,
and, upon reaching the city where Constantine ruled,
sped to meet the emperor.
Constantine had been on the terrace of Blachernae Palace;

there he and George Sphrantzes had surveyed the city.
The angel, upon his decent,
did take on the form of a young watchman,
and in this form
approached the pensive Constantine with God's words:[25]
"Do you not see on the horizon what the pagan has done?
Look toward the strait that
does lead to the Black Sea.
Act quickly, great Constantine, God's regent on earth,
for the great pagan Mehmet
has cut your throat."
"What, lad, do you speak of?" Constantine asked.
"Look, great Constantine,
God's regent on earth, look to the north.
Look, and you will see,
your throat has been cut."
The vile Mehmet had deceived the emperor
and had broken the treaty.
The treachery ran deep, and the antichrist had acted.
The shadow of his unholy empire
cast itself over the hills of Constantinople,
flanked on either side, the holy city
held only the centerpiece of what it once was.
And now Mehmet had seen it fit to break the laws,
and so he built on Roman soil.
To the north of Pera,[26] where the strait did lead to the Black Sea
and where many galleys of the Latin kingdoms passed,
Mehmet had begun his treachery.
Blackened walls now rose up on the shore of Europe,
and the shadow began to thicken,
shrouding the holy light cast down from Gabriel
in dark fumes of pagan lust.
The throat cutter of Constantine, a fortress,
a statue of unholy grandeur,
clutched at the throat of the poor Romans.[27]
With God's words in his heart, strong-armed Constantine,

most righteous Constantine,
confronted the antichrist:
"You most treacherous beast Mehmet—
you who have broken the old law
and desire to spark conflict so that you may fulfill
your hatred for God's sons
and satisfy your pagan deity—
how could I have believed that a pagan could keep his word?
Forgive me, God, and watch over me, that justice can be had.
Mehmet, retract your vile ambitions;
you have no right to build on the soil
our Lord God granted us,
for with this fortress you do strangle me,
and the Latins,[28] and God.
Retract your vile ambitions, cast your spires
built from the stones of hell
to the ground,
and do not spark an unnecessary war.
Retract your vile ambitions, and may Lord God
forgive you and your pagan ways."
Mehmet, God's shadow, responded to the great lord Constantine:
"Do not make me laugh, nonbeliever.
Do not make me ridicule your weak hand,
which cannot even hold together the
small province you call Rome.
Your empire contains but a city:
beyond the fosse you have no dominion and own nothing.
If I wish to build my great fortress at the mouth
of the great trade routes, I shall, and
no one, not even your false god, can forbid me."[29]
Fear did grip Constantine
and those living within Theodosian's protection,
who now saw from the walls
the great devises of the Turks being made.

Send Aid, Franks, Lest the Great City Fall

And so Constantine prayed and sent word unto the Latin states
that they might aid their Christian brothers of the East.
But the Franks would remain as treacherous as the Turks
and would be slow to reply.
Only a bold few would come to Constantine's call,
those who too heard the voice of God
and deemed to protect His empire
from the coming infidels.
But not before the infidels struck and from their fortress
spread like a disease.
Pouring forth like bees from a disturbed hive,
the pagans swarmed from the gates of the Throat Cutter,
and there they deemed
to make havoc on Roman soil.
On the grand pagan Mehmet's command,
the Turks struck at the Roman villages,
and there they committed many vile acts.

And the emperor could do nothing but await aid
as his people burned in pagan fury.
Constantine called upon God and called upon the messenger Gabriel
that the wrongdoings should be stopped.
He cried to the one shrouded in clouds, cried to the setting sun,
and sought refuge in his quarters—that he may not witness
more horror from outside Theodosian's protection.
It had begun: the world began to collapse in on Constantine;
it was as if the apocalypse had come,
and the angels of death sought the soul of the brave emperor,
who would have so willingly sallied forth from the Golden Gate
and on the plains of Rome do battle with the pagan Mehmet,
and there find victory like his fathers before him,
had only the Romans been ready for such a challenge.
The bees of Mehmet desecrated houses of worship,
pillaging the sacred sights outside the walls,
destroying the images of God and His saints,
stealing the beauty that decorated their columns.
Brave Romans of the fields
attempted to end the sack and confronted the pagans,
but were only run through by curved blades.
They would find their way into heaven;
God would see to it.
Brave Constantine, strong-armed son of Heraclius himself,
with words strong and pure, confronted Mehmet:
"I take refuge in God.[30]
If God wishes this city to fall, then let His will be done,
but I will continue to fight for the inhabitants of my city
built in His name
with all my strength.
Let those treaties which were bound by my oath dissolve,
now that you have broken them.
Henceforth I will keep the city gates closed.
May God pass righteous judgment and
decide the outcome of this conflict,

now that you have preferred war over peace."[31]
Mehmet, great and evil king of the pagans, struck again:
to make an example of the Latins,
who might come to Constantine's aid,
and to inspire fear in the hearts of the brave Christians.
Mehmet put the Throat Cutter
into use.
A Latin vessel of Venice, all brave men aboard,
upon arrival from the Black Sea
did try to surpass the Throat Cutter and fulfill
its mission to Constantinople.
Stones cast from the fiery throats of the dragons[32]
skipped across the sparkling water;
for brief moments it was like a simple play-thing of a child
who does skip pebbles along a river
with a desire to have the pebble reach the other side.
But unlike the pebble of a child,
the stones of the dragons
plunged deep into the heart of the vessel,
splintering the galley and the men within.
At the bottom of the sea it now lies, the Venetian vessel,
first of the Latins to feel Mehmet's evil.
The great commander of the vessel, Antonio Rizzo, so brave
in the face of the heathens,
fell to the hands of the great pagan.
Had he only been left to drown with his comrades,
he might have suffered a less awful fate!
But lo, there was nothing that could be done,
and the brave Antonio Rizzo
was impaled through the anus[33]
and put on display so that fear now struck into the hearts of
the Latins and the Romans who stood by their side.
And now the Latins could do nothing
but weep for their comrades
and hope their seaport homes sent aid;

Constantine spoke: "Behold, friends, it has begun.
I fear for my people, I fear for the empire,
I fear for you, my brother George Sphrantzes,
and the Latins who have suffered such a horrible fate.
We shall give them no quarter, now they have showed us none.
May these pagans once more learn of Roman metal,
and may they burn in hell once
they have been dispatched from this world
by our blades, and by God's will!"

Those Who Came to Constantine's Side

But he would not be alone, the great man
worthy of the name Palaeologus.
And although many of his pleas would return unanswered
from the Franks and Slavs,[34]
and although the Catholics
would be reluctant to answer to
the call of an Orthodox—[35]
Pope Nicholas quivering in his cold throne—
and although the emperor's brothers were being detained in the Morea,[36]
God would send aid, and behind Constantine
they would stand strong,
steadfast, and resolute.
What becomes of a Christian if he is to not aid his brothers?
What becomes of a Christian who does not uphold his faith?
What becomes of God, if the Christians do not act as His children?
What becomes of all those who beneath God seek refuge
but, in the workings of the world,

cast themselves apart from their duties as God's sons?
Stop, and listen.
The song of those who held true to their faith
and came to Constantine's side:
The Genoese, noble Latins, sailed to the city;
with two great galleons, they offered help.
Stepping forth from the wooden vessels,
seven hundred men in full armor,
confident and brave, brought with them
many excellent devices and machines of war.
And among them was the noblest and most venerable of the Latins,
a man who commanded immense respect
and was a hero among his people.
Giovanni Giustiniani Longo, bravest of the Genoese,
had fought countless battles;
his blood was thick with the strength his family wielded,
and he would see to the defense of the city.
There too came people of notable worth,
men who had proved themselves worthy in the face of an enemy
and proved their faith in God
by coming to Constantine's city.
The brothers Bocchiardo came,
Troilo, Paolo, and Antonio,
faithful to their seaport home of Genoa,
faithful to God as they brought with them,
at their own expense,
a strong band of water-logged heroes.
There was a man of Castile,
Don Francisco of Toledo, a man of strong stature
who would stand by Constantine's side
in the struggle that was to come.
From Catalonia came a band of strong men; they too
had proved themselves in combat.
And do not forget another great man who came to the city,
John Grant of Germany,[37] who like the Latin brothers

came at his own expense.
He knew all workings of engines and mechanisms
and would be valuable
in the defense of the city.
But those who came to aid the Romans,
although strong and worthy and faithful,
were few in number,
and the king of the Catholics had not come.
George Sphranzes mourned: "Witness, Constantine,
the Catholic's treachery;
a disgrace in the eyes of God, they have not come
to defend His city.
Instead they choose to ignore His plight,
and may God punish them for this perjury.
We have received as much aid from Rome
as have been sent by the Sultan of Cairo."[38]
"Do not mourn, George, but look who has come,
look at these noble people who have come to our aid,
who have found it in their hearts
to lock shields with us
and defend against the pagans," answered the emperor.
"Great Constantine, you speak true;
forgive me for my failing heart."
The brave son of Longo
immediately showed his worth upon arriving,
and being so wise in the art of wall fighting,
began the preparation of the city
so that it might once again shine as proud as it did
in the days when the Persians knelt
defeated at the gates.
The fosse, which had halted the hordes of so many
who wished to see the city fall,
had fallen out of use, and Giustiniani would see to it
that the earth which now filled it
was quickly dispatched of.

He would also see to the crumbling edges of the walls
and restore them to their previous strength,
and like the gates of heaven
they would sparkle.

The Bees Spill from the Hive

Sing of the pagans who marched from hell's gates.
Sing of God's tears that did flow
when the pagans fixed their eyes
on His city.
They came in droves, moving with swiftness
unnatural to the attributes of normal men,
and from all corners of the pagan empire they came;
who can describe the numbers who rallied to the pagan cause?
From the rocky Tokat and the hilled Sivas they came;
from the forested Kemach and Erzurum,
to the river-riddled Ganga and Bayburt,
Trabzon, Bursa, and Edirne they rallied.[39]
Like a serpent of steel, an endless river of hearts bent on destruction,
flaming with hatred, they set out;
so the serpent glowed red with lust and ambition,
and the pagans, as numerous as stones at the bottom of a brook,
laughed in glee at the thought
that they would sack the great city and
bathe in riches stained with holy blood.

On the pagan holy day, the serpent came from its hole;
the head of it was Mehmet, whose eyes sparkled
at the sight of Constantine's city.
And when the serpent assembled outside Theodosian's walls,
behold Thermopylae:
three hundred Spartans in the face of a million Persians.[40]
The Muslims assembled before the walls;
in their center stood the vile Mehmet amongst his demons.
The White Turbans, the feared Janissaries, stood at his side;
they were the products of terrible rule by the sultans,
and may God help the Christians at Constantinople
should they suffer a similar fate
as that which faced the Janissaries.
Taken while still young, born in the image of God,
they became the sultan's slaves
after their families were ravished by the sultan's men.
And now in their hearts they are as cruel as Mehmet,
and blindly they abide by his will.
How distraught the Christians were when they saw
fellow Christians assembled beneath the great pagan.
From the Slavic nations, these poor creatures
have forsaken the path of God,
and in their fear have taken up
the curved blade of the Turks,
their starved families
awaiting great wealth only a sacking would entail.
The unholy treacherous lord of Mehmet, Karaja Pasha,
a brutal man who had risen to high rank
through torture and murder,
held these slaves under his will, and he would
lead them to the walls to do battle with the brave sons of Romulus,
who would do well to kill such a man,
who, born Roman, did turn
to the false god of the pagans.
Ishak Pasha and Mahmut Pasha were there.

Strong and proud, if they were not such infidels
they would have made great lords among men.
Instead they brought with them
those of the eastern corners of the unholy empire,
and under a banner painted red
they faced Theodosian's strong arm.
When does one weep in the face of such terror?
How does one summon the courage when all seems lost?
How did the pagans muster such fury
to pose such threat to the Romans?
But sing no more of the vile pagans who stood at heaven's gates.
The thirteenth of April in the year of our Lord, 1453,
the Christians assembled in the face of the enemy.
There was Nicephorus Palaeologus, great kin to the emperor,
and he had with him
all fine men dressed for war.
There was Loukas Notaras, the last of the Grand Dukes;
he was himself strong and noble,
surpassed only by the great Constantine
in acts of heroism and loyalty,
and he had with him
all fine men dressed for war.
There was strong-armed Demetrios, brother of Constantine,
who had a love for his brother rivaled only
by his love of the sword,
and he had beside him
all fine men dressed for war.
There was wise Theophilus Palaeologus, upon whose feet
were spurs made of pure gold.
He had spent much time in the Frankish areas of the West
and, like the Western knights of old,
was a man of the horse and of the sword.
He had with him loyal and strong folk from his own house,
all fine men dressed for war.
There was Theodore of Karystes, who was learned

in the many languages of the world,
and he too brought with him
fine men dressed for war.
There were the men from Crete, who had come at the emperor's request
and took up guard at the seawall.
From a tower they would watch that the Golden Horn
did stay secure and could give word to the emperor
if God saw it fit to send aid from the West.
From their tower, the Cretans assembled the great chain;
latching it to the seawall of the city,
they did pull the chain by galley across the Golden Horn
and, with the permission of the Genoese at Pera,
attached the end of the chain to the walls of the Latin colony,
so sealing the city from the sea and protecting the Horn
which was so valuable to the Romans.
True heroism came from the Latins:
the Bocchiardo brothers with their band
secured the palace Blachernae,[41]
but not even their great acts could match those of
Giustiniani of the swift-feet,[42]
the proud man so learned in the arts of wall combat and engines of war,
and with him men equally skillful and well dressed for war.
These Latins stood in the center of the wall, the place called the Mesoteichion[43]
where they waited with the great Constantine,
and stared across the plain at Mehmet
who too held up the center of his army.
And Giustiniani was not alone as noble Constantine brought with him
the strongest of the Romans, his personal guard,
and placed them among the men of Giustiniani.
Such courage strong-armed Constantine had!
He would see to it himself that his city was safe,
noble to the name of Palaeologus,
and would himself confront those who
dared to fight against God.

The Crumbling Stones and the Dragon's Breath

Assembled thus, the two armies did face each other,
a pagan host confronting the armies of God.
And from the pagan host a messenger carried unto the wall
a declaration from the great pagan Mehmet,
who knew the city would not fall without struggle
and thought to instill some fear in the Christians
before the struggle began:
"Under Allah, the great, the most benevolent, my master Mehmet
does call to you, king of the Romans.
If you do choose to surrender your city and your religion
and if your people give up their religion
and submit to the true Faith, Allah the Omnipotent,
then may your city and her people stand,
but under the condition that you pay each year
a hundred gold pieces for every man living within your walls.
Embrace these conditions not,
and each one of you will die

and your souls will never reach paradise."
Constantine struck the messenger down in strife
and sent him back to the great pagan with strong words:
"Let your master, the great infidel,
cast himself against the rocks of the city,
let him bloody his hands with the corpses of his own men,
let him break himself against the strong stones before me, and
let him find his way in hell.
Return to your master and tell him
Romans do not yield to the Philistine."
When the emperor uttered these words,
the known world did collapse,
and with a deafening roar resembling
the heavens being torn asunder,
an unholy blast in a great fury penetrated deep
into the hearts of the Christians,
who cowered behind the walls in this moment of terror.
Those who had stood so proud on the walls of Theodosian
could not help but find themselves
screaming with the coward.
Women wailed in the streets and collapsed upon their knees,
children wept, and old men cringed;
never before had such fear gripped the people,
who sought sanctuary in God's buildings of worship.
At these buildings the populace wept in unison;
here they cried to God:
"Why, God, have you brought this upon us?
Have we not done everything in just measure?
Have we not done everything for You, Lord God?
Do not betray us in the end to Your enemies;
do not destroy Your worthy people;
and do not take away Your loving kindness from us
and render us weak at this time!"[44]
For it was in this moment that the vile Mehmet did unleash the dragons[45]
upon the walls of the Christians,

and in a crack of dust and smoke and ash,
Theodosian's wall began to crumble.
Who can describe the terror that did wreck the hearts of the Romans?
An unholy flame came with a hellish thunder,
a thunder which threatened to cast the world into pieces,
leaving gaping holes in the surface of the earth,
stones falling to the depths of hell,
bringing the Romans down with them.
A blast so great frothed from the throat of the metal beast,
and Constantine himself, one who did not know fear like normal men,
who had so many times before
faced the fiercest of foes and did not fail to fell each one,
now knew the true nature of fear.
A fear gripped the hearts of all,
and it can be said
that even God in His palace above the clouds
felt fear as well.
"The apocalypse has come!" cried the people.
The outermost part of Theodosian's wall thus began to collapse,
the wall which since the days of Saint Constantine[46] had not been breached
and which since the old days
had not bent to the will of the either the Sassanids or Slavs,
Arabs, Mameluks, Rus, Franks,[47] or Bulgars—
in the swiftness of a small fall breeze
bent to the will of the sons of Osman and Orhan.
But although the Turks would bend the will of Theodosian,
it would not be enough to bend the will of the Romans,
who in Constantine's presence no longer feared
but were inspired by his love for his people
and stood up against the thundering of hell.

The Swift-Footed
Before the Wall

Brave, fleet-footed Giustiniani!
The grand Genoese acted with haste
and brought to the fallen parts of the wall
a new way devised to block the breach.
With wood and earth and cloth, skins and stone,
fleet-footed Giustiniani
built a second wall to replace that which had fallen,
and once again the wall was strong,
and once again the Romans
were steadfast in the eyes of the pagan.
And the dragons sounded;
a constant thunder shook the world and all men's senses,
but Giustiniani would never grieve.
He saw his wall collapse in the thunder,
the skins and stones and wood cracking,
the earth giving way to the great stones
which dared enter the city.

Giustiniani watched his wall fall;
time and time again he saw his work fail.
Each day the wall failed,
and each night it was made anew,
so the pagans angered
when they saw their stones falling short.
And when the stones failed, the men were sent:
beneath a rain of spears and steel, the Red Turbans[48] came,
which from the wall looked like a red stream of blood
that did make its way to the wall,
but crashed upon the rocks of the fosse
and the earth of Giustiniani's palisade,
where they were unable to proceed.
There, before the fosse and the earth wall,
the river of red turbans became a river of real blood;
there before the city,
the pagans and Christians met and did exchange blows.
Each day for six nights the wall fell.
Each night for six days it was rebuilt.
Each day for six nights the fosse was taken.
Each night for six days the fosse was retaken.
For six days the pagans died before the city of Constantine,
and for six days Constantine wept.
And before dawn of the seventh day,
Giustiniani called out Karaja Pasha: "Come, pagan!
He who seeks the end of the Romans, I seek your end;
let our blades decide this day."
Karaja Pasha was no coward and stepped to Giustiniani in challenge,
and between the two armies they fought
to decide the fate of the battle.
Giustiniani broke the flowered shield of Karaja Pasha,
a blow which no byrnie[49] could impede,
and clove the pagan in half,
flinging him dead over a small bush.[50]
And the pagans fled from the wall, and the Christians cheered.

Giustiniani stepped over the cloven pagan body and spoke:
"We have won the land battle of six long days;
hold steady and praise God for this victory,
He who decided to be gracious
in this moment of struggle.
But look to the seawall, where our brothers
still hold off the pagan fleet."
And on the seventh day, the Christians rested.

May the Sea Swallow
Mehmet's Slaves

The Great Pagan had done an impossible deed
and had assembled a great fleet,
which upon the seas rough and calm
did threaten the Christians.
The seas that had held the empire intact
were now at the mercy of the pagan fleet,
which could not have been constructed
without the aid of hellish beasts,
for with a swiftness the fleet approached
the seawalls of Constantinople,
and on the first day of the land struggle,
the struggle for the sea began.
Assembling behind the safety of the great chain,
the fleet of the Christians prayed to God
that the sea would swallow the pagan fleet.
But the pagan fleet which held a most brutal slave of Mehmet,
the vile Baltaoglu,[51] was not swallowed by the sea

and with trumpets and drums
threatened the Golden Horn.
The Great Zorzi Doria of Genoa assembled his fleet
the span from Pera to Constantinople,
and there they waited to join battle with Baltaoglu.
The Turks, with their Christian slaves rowing at full pace,
launched the fleet at the boom.
Castanets, drums, horns, bugles, screams, cries:
the arrival of the devils.
Preceding the awful clash, both sides let loose javelins and arrows,
stones from the sling and flames from heaven,
cries holding the spirits high;
fighting for God, the great Christians held strong
when the two fleets came together.
On the seawalls the defenders of the city cheered their brothers on,
watching as brave Zorzi Doria himself fought amongst
many pagans who did encircle him.
And across the walls the clergy assembled,
parading the great icons of the city and of Holy God,
singing great psalms to inspire His soldiers,
so that the sailors might find salvation
and keep the Turks at bay.
And upon felling his fifth foe, Zorzi Doria inspired his men:
"Look, brave sailors! Look to our wall!
Our friends watch our struggle!
The Holy Ones aid our fight!
Press, men, press, and let not the pagans through this line.
God shall grant us victory!"
And the three hundred Spartans echoed, "God shall grant us victory!"
Abreast the boom, it was as if
there was no longer water.
The bodies of vessels and the bodies of men
now encircled the battle where the water should have been,
and the Golden Horn ran red.
And as the land wall held for six days,

the boom was defended from the pagans.
And on the seventh day the evil Baltaoglu fled,
forced to flee from the frenzied fray,
the pagans at his heels,
back to the safety of the northern coasts.
And the water-borne Christians rested.

Aid From Heaven

Constantine gave thanks to God for the victory;
the initial strike had been repelled,
but he knew Mehmet would never yield
until each and every pagan sent to fight
lay dead before the wall.
But on that day the greatest of events stirred the heart of the son of Manuel,[52]
for his prayers would be answered.
On the southern horizon, the Latins once again showed their worth,
and vessels were seen from the walls,
approaching the city with a great swiftness,
the red cross on a white field:
the flag of the Genoese.
Four great galleys, a gift from the Senate of Genoa,
a gift from God who deemed to aid the struggle of the Christians.
The people of the city thanked God,
spirits never failing them.
But Mehmet, too, saw the coming of the Genoese
and feared their arrival,
that their coming would impede his success.

Mehmet dispatched once again the slave Baltaoglu in fury:
"Go, and do not fail me again.
Take these sailing ships and kill these Latins,
and should you fail in this task,
do not return alive, for you shall suffer a worse fate
than that which these infidels will suffer
when I storm the city."
And one hundred vessels sailed to oppose the Genoese,
who did not expect such a tragic welcome.
One hundred ships encircled the four galleys,
and the battle for the sea began anew,
and never did the strong-armed Genoese falter.
They continued to harness the wind in the direction of the boom,
where they would find safety with the Christian fleet,
but the pagans did not fail
to attempt Mehmet's will.
From the walls it seemed as if a dry patch of land[53] moved north,
so numerous were the pagans who encircled God's aid.
But the wind became weak, and the Genoese no longer
moved to the safety of the Golden Horn.
And the pagans pressed, and many men died.
And the struggle drifted to the opposite shore,
where more pagans, in anticipation,
waited to destroy the brave Genoese
should the failing wind bring them to heathen soil.
It was as if God had abandoned the Christians after
His initial will to help.
Closer and closer the sea battle drifted toward the shore.
Closer and closer the Genoese came to a certain fate,
but never did the Genoese give ground,
and their four galleys held firm
against the swarm of pagan vessels about them.
And when the moment seemed to come
when the Genoese would be pushed against the eastern shore
where waited the pagans,

God renewed His will to help the Christians.
A wind blew again,
picking up from the south, it spread across the water
and the Genoese harnessed the wind in their sails,
guiding the vessels toward the boom.
Baltaoglu did not relinquish his pursuit of the Latins
until they approached the boom
and the Christian fleet welcomed the Genoese
and pushed Baltaoglu back into the open water.
On the walls and in the Horn,
the Christians cheered,
watching the pagan fleet flee
and granting thanks to the Genoese,
who brought to the city many strong men
and great quantities of grain.
Constantine approached the noble Zorzi Doria,
who disembarked from his vessel;
he was bloodied and grim,
but at the sight of Constantine of the hoary-white beard,
he gladdened.
Constantine kissed him on the forehead and mouth.
"God wishes us success, great lord of Genoa;
we welcome you here with open hearts;
if only were the Turks not at our gates,
a great feast would await your arrival."
Zorzi Doria looked past the wall to the pagan shore.
"Look, great Constantine,
the pagans turn against themselves;
great success this will bring."
For on the pagan shore Baltaoglu returned alive and in shame,
for twice he failed the vile Mehmet,
and he could only be called courageous
in his decision to return to the great sultan,
who promised a harsh punishment.
And the great sultan with his golden shoes

kicked the humbled slave Baltaoglu
into the waters of the Bosphorus.
Baltaoglu could only whimper and plead with Allah
that he would make it to paradise,
for the great sultan would not listen.
By the ships of the pagan fleet, in clear view of the city
Baltaoglu had a metal pole fixed in his anus,
which was then hammered until it reached his throat.
And there by the ships he was hoisted up so to give warning
to those who failed Mehmet.
So was the will of such a vile pagan.

Hold Fast, Romans,
the Pagan's Fury

By the twenty-first day of April,
the great sultan called his slaves to his side.
In the courtyard of the Throat Cutter they spoke
about their failed plan to take the city.
"Look to the south, fellow sons of Allah.
Look and you will see the city still standing;
these nonbelievers still think they can hold up
to Allah's will.
The land wall is thick, and each spot our cannons break through
is plugged with matter so to recreate the wall.
The seawalls cannot be breached;
the currents threaten to dash our vessels against the stones.
Our victory lies in the taking of the Horn;
the Horn is our gateway to the city."
Ishak Pasha, who had been at the wall when the pagans
had been repulsed by Giustiniani,
bowed to the grand sultan. "Sire, Baltaoglu was more able

than any of us in the workings of naval war,
and he failed to take the Horn.
How then can we press the boom?"
And Mehmet showed no sign of fear, for he had pondered
while Baltaoglu's blood
still stained his own hands.
One million Saracens rose to the bidding of Mehmet,
who pressed his men into service.
The Christian hope had risen since Zorzi Doria sailed into the harbor,
but nothing could prepare these brave souls
for the hellish cunning that Mehmet put into effect.
In the shadow of Pera,
the pagans set to work;
like a colony of rats they did the impossible.
On the eve of that day, when Constantine embraced Zorzi Doria,
a parade of hell broke the calm air,
broke the hearts of the Christians who
had sensed God's safety.
A true parade of the underworld emerged,
from the shadow of the Genoese walls,
a strange event not even the wisest of the Romans understood.
George Sphrantzes, who had seen the old days of the empire,
shivered upon the sight of this parade.
What horror did tear at the hearts of the Romans!
Hell itself had risen to aid the Saracens and confront the Christians.
From the shadow of the Genoese walls,
vessels built for the sea
glided across the rocky earth.
Hundreds of them, with flags of many colors,
surrounded by devils who controlled the vessels,
sailed across solid ground
toward the walled city of God.
The drums of hell rang out with
the unnatural parade,
ships which harnessed rock and sailed upon them

as if they sailed the sea![54]
And when they reached the shore of the Horn,
they once again became sea-borne vessels
and sailed into the Christian waters.
Constantine, upon seeing this horrible sight,
called his finest men,
the Latins with their knowledge of the workings of sea-war.
Zorzi Doria and Giacomo Coco were there,
ready to aid the great Constantine in his plight
against hell.
These great Latins spoke advice to the emperor,
casting down their gauntlets with stern faces and
making the sign of the cross above their hearts:
"Lord, without the aid of the boom,
the great chain to divide the force of the pagans,
there can be no victory
against such numbers as they have mustered
from the halls of Aeries.
When night falls, let us and the fleet
approach in silence,
and with the fire of the Greeks,
let us burn these pagans and their unholy vessels."
Constantine embraced them both.
"Go, brothers of the Latin States,[55]
I will pray for your success in Saint Sophia."
And on the third night after that day,
the Latins swiftly sliced the still waters of the Horn.
With a hundred men they approached the pagan vessels,
and it seemed the pagans would fail.
Giacomo Coco called to the men of his vessel
that they might claim glory over the pagans: "Come!
Brave brothers of Genoa, let us take to the vanguard
so that we may be first among those to slay these beasts
And claim the prize their vessel will offer!"
Across the water at Pera,

the city seemed to sleep as
darkness clutched the colony.
But the Latins there did not sleep
but listened to the Christian advance.
The blackness was then disturbed;
on the walls a single light shone.
Lo! Judas amongst the citizens of Pera!
One who had betrayed the faith of his seaport home,
one who had betrayed his faith in the face of Allah!
A light, a light on the tower of Pera!
Alarming the Turks of the coming of God's sons,
the Turks who then turned their cannons unto the Christian vessels.
Hold, brave Latins!
But in the face of a traitor there could be no victory,
and the stones of the cannons
tore through the bones of Coco,
tore through the bones of the vessel,
a hole left in the heart of these Christian souls.
What misery the Latins felt,
and Constantine felt it too,
the loss of his brothers,
whilst in the Great Church.
And he wept as Coco was consumed by water of the Horn
and blood of his men
swirled in circles about him.
And only had he died this great death
would God have preserved his body,
but the waters for once seemed unkind to the Latins
and failed to consume Coco and many of his men,
who found themselves at Mehmet's mercy,
washed up on the shore of the pagans.
There on the pagan shore,
Mehmet greeted the water-weary Latins
with a great fury.
Giacomo Coco knew his fate

and upon looking at the pagan
spat on his feet.
And on that hour,
one hundred Latins,[56] like the pagan Baltaoglu
and like Antonio Rizzo,
were impaled through the anus and lifted
so that the Christians
could see their men die.
And Constantine continued to weep,
as did the Latins who watched their men suffer,
and only thoughts of revenge kept them from
blindly leaping from the walls
to pull their men down from the poles.
Revenge the Christians did have against the pagans
and those Turks taken as prisoners from the passed battles;
three hundred in all
had ropes tied around their necks
and were hanged from the wall so that Mehmet
turned away with deep sorrow and anger.
But God in His lofty seat bathing in the clouds
did not approve of this,
as taking revenge can bring only more sorrow.
The Christians had forgotten in their fury
to turn the other cheek,[57]
and thus He saw it fit
to leave the Romans to the workings of the world
to atone for their sins.[58]
And then Mehmet put his victorious fleet to work,
taking the spars, which carry the sails,
and tying them with strong ropes
made great bridges protected with hides
so that his men did not fear the quarrel
of crossbow or arrow.[59]
These great bridges
spanned the gap between the pagan ships and the wall,

and the Saracens climbed to the battlements.
It was only with great suffering
that God's men repulsed the pagans,
for spears and stones
merely broke on the shields of the attackers.
Only when flames were cast down on the bridges
were the Christians able to see to it
that the Saracens fell down to their doom
in a great rush of water and fire.
Only then the Romans could rest
and peacefully pray the pain
would dissolve with the
screams of the dying.

Great Constantine, What Courage Lays in Your Heart!

With a fury that blinded the Christians,
    they had done a most unholy act,
an act that mimicked the likes of the pagans.
For when the fury cleared their eyes,
they saw the heathens hanging from the walls
and wept at their awful, un-Christian deed.
And the times seemed bleak for the Christians,
for Constantine, who saw his city close
to that which he feared most.
The Horn was now in the hands of the heathens;
on two sides the Christians were now threatened.
Cannons battered the sea and land walls,
the men of God fell beneath falling rock,
and many lost heart.
So the lords of men among the Christians,
on the third day of May,
brought themselves together in the halls of Constantine,

where they would discuss what their failing hearts feared.
Chivalrous Theophilus was there, as was strong-armed Demetrios,
Nicephorus the kin of Constantine, humble Notaras,
John the German, and Don Francisco.
There also stood learned Theodore of Karystes,
swift-footed Giustiniani with a bloodied face,
and the Latin brothers,
Troilo, Paolo, and Antonio,
the blood of Bocchiardo still strong.
George Sphrantzes led Constantine into the hall,
where these powerful men met him and embraced him.
And Constantine seated himself among his lords
and spoke to them: "Tell me, friends, of what we must do."
And Notaras spoke first, so wise he was:
"Now these Saracens have taken the Horn,
we cannot hold out
as long as we have hoped."
Notaras continued to speak, but was overrun
by Demetrios, who burst thus: "Flee, brother!
Flee, great Constantine, that the pagans may not
lay a hand on you!
To Chios or Italy, to the forests of the Franks!
Let not these Saracens have you suffer the same fate
we have witnessed with Giacomo Coco,
Antonio Rizzo, and even Baltaoglu!"
Constantine looked upon his brother. "It saddens me,
brave brother, to see your failing heart.
And listen, all you great lords,
men who have proved their loyalty countless times,
speak no more of this matter of flight,
for never would I dream to abandon
all that these pagans wish to destroy.
If I did flee this city, what would become of the clergy,
the churches of God, the empire, and
all my people?

What, my good friends,
would the world think of me?"[60]
Instead, let us turn to that which we must defend;
look to the walls, look to the next wave
of Turks, who will not rest until all of us Christians
lay dead before God."
And the next wave came
as the cannons which had not ceased to pummel
the walls since the first day
breached a hole where Giustiniani's men stood.
There atop the rubble the Red Turbans advanced
and met the Latins, Giustiniani at their front.
He called, the great Latin of Genoa,
mustering his men to confront the pagans,
and Constantine was there too;
true to his word he fought alongside his men.
So many died on that day,
the Christians never once giving ground
to the swarming Red Turbans.
So many died on that day
that the bodies of those Turks
resembled a bridge or stairway to the city.[61]
Murat the Janissary, a man with the strength
equal to ten of his own men,
took to the front of his line
and held his red-pennoned spear toward Giustiniani
in challenge.
And when these two great lords met in the center of both armies,
an awful clash rang out, and all surrounding men
stopped their combat to look on,
their leaders caught up in a great struggle.
And the Red Turbans roared with glee
when it seemed their master Murat
would triumph.
Murat, with his pennoned spear,

thrust it through the shield of Giustiniani,
and it would have continued through
the mail and flesh of the great Latin
had God not pitied the fine Giustiniani
that the Latin should live.
Gabriel, from the heavens, again parted the clouds,
and upon taking the form of a Greek soldier,
came to Giustiniani's aid
and clove the leg of Murat so that the pagan could stand no more,
relinquishing his grip on the Latin,
falling amongst the many dead beneath the rubble.[62]
But look to the east, Romans!
There the great Theodore of Karystes, the speaker of many languages,
locked with the flag bearer Omar Bey,
ruthless pagan he was and valuable to the cause of Mehmet.
If only Omar Bey could be dispatched of,
the pagan banner would fall,
and the Romans could rest that day.
And fortune did shine on the Romans,
when Theodore broke his sword
on the helm of the pagan
and flung him dead off the wall,
where the Saracens could gather their fallen.
So the pagans fled from the walls that day,
but the Christians did not rejoice,
so weary and sad they were.

The Failing Faith

There at the Mesoteichion the battle continued to be had.
There in the breach atop the rubble,
the Romans dwindled in number,
holding to the waves of pagans
that cascaded upon them.
Like the current of the Bosphorus,
the pagan waves ebbed and flowed,
a never ending current,
a current bringing only further death,
only further suffering upon Constantine's brow.
And Mehmet seemed unaffected by
the loss of lives,
for innumerable pagans had fallen,
and never did he shed a tear.
Instead he sent his demons on, so that
the current never abated
but only grew stronger and more brutal
as he put new workings into effect.
With towers of war, he pressed the walls of the city,[63]

and the Romans never gave.
At the walls, Mehmet had his men whipped so that
his pagans never fled in the face
of the furious Romans.[64]
Constantine, ever present at the walls, saw to it
that the Romans never succumbed,
even when the pagans seemed to sprout from
the very earth with the desire
to surpass the wall.
It was here that the great German John Grant
showed his worth to the Christian cause.
Beneath the wall itself, like rats the pagans made holes,
spreading beneath Theodosian like a plague,
emerging where the Romans took their rest.
Deep in the darkness amongst the worms
the German fought these rats;
beneath the very feet of Constantine,
the battle raged in candlelight.
And the German never failed the emperor,
collapsing the earth upon the pagans
so that they did suffocate beneath the walls.[65]
And further did the number of Romans dwindle,
but still they would not give ground.
On the fiftieth day of the siege, sadness and despair
tore at the hearts of the Christians,
for even though they had not bowed to the pagans,
it seemed as if the apocalypse had come,
that God had abandoned the Christians
to the cruel makings of the world,
that he had left them
in the shadow of death.
On the first hour of that day, the Christians awoke,
and only whiteness covered them.
But not a whiteness like the heavens,
an eerie white of death,

a white the color of bones left after a feast.
And so thick it was the Christians could not see,
so pale and deathly white it was,
engulfing the figures of the Romans.
And when it seemed this fog would lift,
it was only replaced by a red haze,
blood-soaked clouds drifting through the streets,
filling the mouths and nostrils and eyes of the people,
muffling voices and cries.
When this haze lifted, it left behind its bloodiness,
a red taint on the roofs of the buildings,
on the stones of the paved streets,
so that the world looked bloodstained.
The great church of Saint Sophia looked as if
a butcher had done his work across its tiles,
and the Romans wept at this sight.
Loukas Notaras came forth to the people
and spoke with great mourning to the clergy:
"Look, people!
What has become of our city?
For so thick this evil haze is, I cannot see from my hand
to the Holy Apostles!
God, why do you forsake us?
Great servants of the Lord, bring that which can protect us,
the Hodegetria,[66] that it may aid us in this struggle!"
And the clergy brought forth the Hodegetria,
and the black- robed procession
began in the streets of the city.
There the clergy were joined by the people,
those who could not wield weapons—
the young, the old, the women, the children—
song ringing between the people,
calls to God and the Mother Mary.
In the streets, prayer gave hope to the people,
the song sweeping up the hearts of the men on the walls,

the incense of the censers waking men from
their nightmarish slumber beneath and atop the walls.
"Do thou save thy city, as thou knowest and willest!
We put thee forward as our arms, our rampart, our shield, our general:
do thou fight for thy people," [67] they sang.
Who can speak then, of the evil deed that followed?
For on that hour, the Hodegetria, which did top the procession,
by a force unseen by the eyes of those watching,
fell from its altar and fixed itself
onto the paved stone road below. [68]
Who can explain this happening?
For not one of the Romans
could pull from the ground this great edifice,
and it stayed fixed against the stones.
Loukas Notaras spoke: "Oh, God, do You not pity us?
Oh, God, do You leave us to die amongst these pagans?"
And the Roman people,
prying at the edges of the Hodegetria,
called forth after the Duke, "Oh God,
do You leave us to die amongst these pagans?"
And He answered:
Light streaked across the sky,
and the heavens rained and hailed with such might
that through the streets came rivers from the clouds
sweeping women and children along the paved streets,
and the procession dissolved as the people fled to their homes.
And when the rain and hail stopped,
the people once again emerged into the streets
only to behold more terror.
Looking upon the still stained bloodied roof of Saint Sophia,
the people screamed in anguish at what they saw.
A flame illuminated in the upper story.
For a moment it appeared as if the roof had been set alight,
and many feared the Turks had entered the city.
But the flame did not consume the great church;

instead it came together with an awful rush

and streaked upwards,

parting the clouds with light

and disappearing thereafter.[69]

The people in the streets, humble Loukas Notaras among them,

shrieked and tore out their hair:

"God has abandoned us!

His light has fled our great church!

Alas what horror shall befall us!

The city is doomed!"

And the people cast down their faith.

But Constantine did not fail even when God, Himself,

deemed the city should fall.

Instead he rallied his troops by the walls,

stood by their sides, and gave them words of courage

that the city should never be abandoned,

that the last man should die in defiance.

Alas! It was too late for the brave Constantine.

The heathens sent forth a decorated emissary

to speak terms to the emperor,

when it now seemed certain

the city would suffer a horrible fate.

The emissary spoke to Constantine,

who sat alongside his friend George Sphrantzes,

his three hundred Spartans about him,

listening to the final moments of their empire:

"Emperor Constantine Palaeologus,

it seems your God has abandoned you,

you who can no longer defy us.

Submit now, fallen king, last of the Romans,

and grant the grand Sultan Mehmet your city,

now that it is clear who will triumph."

And Constantine furrowed his brow,

seated among his brave people,

who all carried numerous wounds, and

looked to the eyes of the pagan.
"It is not in my power
to hand over the city.
But before its walls will I die among my men,
before I see a single heathen enter my city."
And the pagan left,
back to the great Sultan Mehmet,
and the Christians prayed,
awaiting the final moments in defiance
and in mourning.

Romans, Look Upon the Apocalypse, and Be Brave!

That night, the twenty-eighth day of May,
the fate of the city would be decided.
And Constantine was ready for this day
and embraced it with prayer.
Beneath the dome of Saint Sophia,
beneath the image of God who did
look upon the Christians,
the Romans gathered together.
A most mournful ceremony indeed!
At the altar, the men did not shed their armor
but glistened in the candlelight
as they sought God's aid in this final struggle.
Smoke and incense, murmuring prayer,
tears and moans,
who can describe such a moment?
Outside the walls the heathens mustered
a light in the pitch black,

followed by a million more:
the flames of the pagan host.
But the fear, which the pagans intended,
did not reach the hearts of the Romans,
who were now steady in their resolve
to not abandon the city
and to hold the city until the last man.
In his quarters, the emperor dressed in armor,
called his servants and his household men
to his side.
His great bodyguard formed around him,
the feared Varangian Guard: [70]
men from the Western Isles
who carried the weight of centuries of war,
their armor still stained with
the blood of uncountable battles
in the face of the Roman emperors
they had sworn to protect.
And there he pronounced: "My friends, servants of the empire,
forgive me of any hardships
I have imposed upon you.
Forgive me, and let God see righteousness in my actions
and be assured that it was all in His service.
Thank you, and if you are to see the end of this day,
be careful in the eye of the pagan,
for I shall not return to this house,
and after this night,
I will be in God's hands."
The servants replied, "Go, great emperor,
and may fortune find you on the field
where the pagans seek your death."
Constantine rode forth from the palace Blachernae;
he was seen galloping through the streets of the city,
his loyal bodyguard streaming behind him,
calling to all able Romans,

rousing them and pressing them to the wall.
At the Mesoteichion, the emperor stood in front of all those
who would do battle that night.
There he spoke to his men of this last great struggle,
an attempt to instill new hope
after the abandonment of God.
George Sphrantzes stood by his side,
a most noble friend.
He had been there for the emperor at the siege of Patras
and had rescued the young Constantine
beneath the rubble of the city;
he had served for thirty years under the emperor,
had searched the lands for a wife,
and was made godfather of the emperor's children.
And not even in these final hours of the city
would he leave the emperor's side.
Constantine spoke to his three hundred Spartans:
"Great men of Rome!
Great soldiers of God, who have shown courage
beyond all other men!
The final moment has come,
when we all must stand strong together once more.
This heathen Saracen wishes to turn the city of Constantine
to a pen for his sheep,
to replace our places of God
with idols of their false god,
to make your wives slaves of his men
and your children soldiers of the false faith.
Let not our city fall to this!"
Constantine began to weep as he pleaded
with the last of his men, but continued thus:
"Great Latins and Romans,
you have shown your worth;
before the walls you have not faltered.
So stand strong one last time,

and before the arms of Theodosian,
let us do battle with these pagans,
and if God has seen it fit that
this city should fall,
let them not forget the Romans of Constantinople,
God's soldiers on earth,
who despite all horrors and death,
despite fiery dragons and red turbans,
never fled!"
The Romans did not cheer but wept,
and each one of them
embraced the emperor in turn
before assembling.
Between the inner and outer walls of the city,
the last weary Romans came together.
There would be no flight;
Giustiniani's wall was at their front,
only the pagan flames visible past this wall,
and the strong inner wall at their back,
locked so that none could flee.
All the great lords were there among their men,
fleet-footed Giustiniani, brave Constantine, learned Theodore,
strong-greaved Theophilius, Don Francisco, young Demetrios, John Grant.
The grand duke Loukas Notaras was not there,
faint-hearted after the departure of God.
And there between the two walls the Romans awaited
the coming heathens.
The world thundered in awful resurrection
of the dragon's flames pounding Giustiniani's wall.
Beneath rubble and stone many Romans fell
but grieved no more,
embracing this final day with their king
who among them offered strong words.
They waited, the Romans, as the stones came.
They waited, the Romans, on the most horrid day

ever to be lived.
They waited, the Romans, for the coming heathens,
so that they might make themselves remembered.
When the final stones fell among the Christians,
the flames of the Turks approached—
the first wave to cascade upon the brave men.
On each front, the pagans crashed upon the Christians,
and they held,
each and every brave soul,
breaking shields and cleaving helms,
the great Constantine with his glistening armor
and gold-pennoned spear
a sight to behold!
With his lords around him, the emperor
pressed the Romans so that the pagans
feared an awful death
at the hand of such a furious foe.
The heathens rang out in song,
if it could be called so,
screeches of the their god and of death—
the song of the coming destruction.
But the Romans did not give in to such horrid song,
but had their hope renewed,
the clergy in chant atop the walls,
the bells of the houses of God in song.
In the face of such furious Christians, the pagans[71]
could not hold,
brutal yet faint-hearted they were.
And the heathens began to break,
even with the chavushes at their rear.
The first wave fled the walls,
but the Christians were allowed no rest.
The sun rose, and the Red Sea now pressed:
the swarm of turbans the color of blood,
the slaves of the Anatolian continent,

tearing at the mail of the defenders,
who again broke the pagans.
And then came Mehmet himself,
a pagan atop a black horse
glittering with such splendor, such fury,
only the strongest of heart did not quiver.
With the great sultan came the feared bodyguard,
those poor Christians who now thrived on
the heathen fury.
And how can one describe what havoc there was at the walls,
how many screamed their last breath,
how many fell beneath the rubble,
how many found their way to heaven.
Among them was the chivalrous Theophilus,
the Roman of the Franks, kin of Constantine,
with golden spurs given to him by
the king Valois himself.
Poor chivalrous Theophilus, such ill-fortune to befall you!
He locked with the pagan Mahmut Pasha
atop the steps the bodies of the fallen
that did bridge the ditch
with Giustiniani's wall.
The pagan clove the shield of the kin of Constantine;
over the rubble the Christian could not keep his feet
after such a blow.
And the brave Theophilus was flung dead
amongst the bodies of the Red Turbans.
There, too, Theodore met his fate.
It was a shame he was more of a scholar
than a soldier
and his valiance did not match
his skill with a sword.
In his attempt to aid his friend Theophilus,
Theodore was met by Ishak Pasha
who clove the helmet of the scholar in two,

and the learned one was no more.
Constantine ailed when he saw his two great friends
fall before the wall
and pressed forward with Giustiniani and the German John Grant
to avenge his fallen brethren.
In the face of the furious Christians,
the pagan lords Mahmut and Ishak tried to flee
but only got so far as the ditch,
where the emperor plunged his spear through mail and flesh
and flung them dead
in the face of the grand Sultan Mehmet.
The eyes of the two great men met,
and the fury of the battle increased,
but the press of men between them meant
they could not yet strike up blows.
The line of the Christians never faltered,
and the exchange of blows began
to favor the defenders of God,
who rained upon the pagans a fiery fury,
such fierce battle unbeknownst to the world,
and it seemed the Spartans would win out the day.
Constantine sensed the faltering Red and White Turbans,
heathens who had never before
fled in the face of the enemy.
He called to his men, the emperor, in a loud voice: "Press, brothers!
See that these heathens fear us!
I know that you are weary!
I know you have seen hell and kept the demons at bay!
Look now as the Turks quiver!
Press now once more, Christians,
and we shall see them take flight;
before God we shall finally break these pagans,
and to the ends of the world we shall pursue them!"
The great emperor urged his men forward;
with the last remnants of strength,

they locked shields with the faltering pagans
and pressed them toward the ditch,
and it seemed the day was won.
Yet despite the efforts of the Christians,
it was not God's will that the Romans
should prevail.
The battlefield strongly lit by the sun suddenly darkened;
and yet it was still daylight hours,
it seemed night had come again.
Who but God can describe such unnatural events?
God's resolve spread across the sun,
telling the Romans of their sin,
calling to the Turks that they might punish
such sinners.
And the Christian people wept up at the sky,
cried in agony at the sight they beheld:
the sultan's banner in the place
of the now blackened sun.[72]

Constantine's Stand

Then, ringing out over the din of the battlefield,
    a heathen stone of iron
from the throat of a dragon
struck deep in the heart of the greatest of men—
Giustiniani, one who none thought could fall,
who atop the rubble commanded the Christians.
Through leather, wood, and mail,
the iron pierced his flesh,
and he fell, fell off the crest of the rubble,
and the Christians embraced his body,
carrying him to the emperor.
The grieving grew worse when the great Latin fell,
Giustiniani, who with faint breath asked the emperor,
"Let me tend to my wound, great king.
Give me the keys to the inner wall, which has been locked
so that we do not flee,
and I shall return when my wound is bound."
The emperor knew to let the great Latin die here
would have all hope left in the Latins' hearts disappear,

and the emperor was kind
and knew Giustiniani was in deep pain.
Brave Constantine! Brave son of Romulus! Kind son of the Romans!
But unfortunate emperor, that the world
does not recognize kindness;
the now godless land is cruel and merciless.
He placed the keys to the lesser gate
in the hand of the ailing Giustiniani,
who with his personal guard moved
with the greatest swiftness the bleeding man could achieve.
Sing, then, of the horror that followed,
the treachery of the Latins, who for so long
stood at the side of the emperor.
But blame we not the godly men of Genoa,
Venice, nor fleet-footed Giustiniani,
who did so well to see the city secured;
the burning crest of the sultan in the sky
would have shrunken the stoutest hearts of men.
For, when the lesser gate opened, the Latins broke,
calling after their lord, "Why do you leave us?
Why do you abandon us in the face of this foul enemy?"
Temptation, temptation flooding the hearts of the Latins,
who saw their lord leave and who saw
the locked gate no longer left unopened.
And streaming from the line of Christians
locked in combat against the numerous bees,
the wretched pagans, the violent infidels,
the Latins ran after their lord.[73]
Constantine knew now that the Lord wished the city to fall,
for in the moment of victory
the tide of the swarming infidels did not ebb
but only increased in fury.
Around him, one by one
the sturdy Varangians
died at the feet of the emperor

CHRISTOPHER IMPIGLIA

like their ancestors before them,
pierced by a thousand spears.
And in this moment Constantine did an unspeakable deed,
an attempt to defy the will of God
and protect the city until the very end.
Rather than succumb to the Lord's bidding,
rather than let the city surrender for their sins,
he spoke to his men in a proud manner:
"Brave Latins, do not flee!
You shall fall, every last one of you, if the line
does not hold.
Lo, that I should not have let brave Giustiniani go!
But that deed is done, so press, men, press,
and do not let these pagans through!"
The heathens had broken through where the Latins
had stood and now advanced to crush
a resistance from the Romans which
would never abate.
Constantine held his gold-pennoned spear
with the German John Grant and Don Francisco at his side,
Demetrios and Nicephorus, who would be with Constantine
until the very end.
And flowing over the rubble the pagans came,
circling the fewer Romans,
who never did lay down their arms.
To the north where the Bocchiardo brothers stood,
at the palace Blachernae, where Constantine
had spent numerous summers in comfort,
the Christians broke.
The strong-armed Latin brothers could do nothing,
as they now lay dead,
cast off the walls onto the rubble below,
their hands still clutching their spears.
The flag of Palaeologus no longer fluttered above the palace;
it was replaced now by the

half moon of the sultan.[74]
The citizens wailed,
the church bells sang;
a song of such mourning was made.
The heathens cheered,
the Christians prayed,
but nothing could be said
to change the tide of the never-ending flood.
For now betwixt the two walls of Theodosian
the Christians died,
trampled beneath the heathen feet.
And once Giustiniani's wall was breached,
there was no stopping the flood,
and the heathens came and let none in their path
breathe a last breath.
Like a cracked bowl lost at the riverside by a small boy,
it will drift down the river, and as it carries along,
the crack will fill with water,
will widen as the water fills its gaps.
Then it is only a matter of moments
before the bowl sinks beneath the surface.
So was the breach in Giustiniani's wall,
and soon the city would submerge.
Constantine could not bear to see his city
in the hands of such heathens,
to see Saint Sophia, the Hippodrome, Blachernae,
crumble under pagan fury,
to see the city that was the centerpiece of the world
lose all that it once was.
And so Constantine looked to John Grant and Don Francisco,
young Demetrios, and strong-greaved Nicephorus,
and spoke to them as he looked on
at the Christian men falling before him:
"Good men, good Christians!
Look now at the true makings of the world;

look now at a world no longer governed by God,
left by Him to the makings of the heathens.
For this is what they seek, these evil sons of Osman,[75]
they seek our end, the end of the world
we have created.
I will not see my city in their hands;
come now with me, my kin Demetrios and Nicephorus,
my good friends, John and Don Francisco.
Let us die with our people,
beneath these very walls which were built by our kin,
let us die with our spears in hand.
But let them not use our bodies as tokens of their victory,
when our spirit is no longer in them
and they lie amongst the rubble.
Let not these heathens desecrate our bodies
and strip from them our armor.
So do as I do, when I pull from my mail
the mark of my rank,
the emblem of my family."
And John, Demetrios, and Nicephorus followed the emperor
and pulled from their mail
the emblems of their rank.
Then they embraced the emperor one by one,
kissed him on the eyes and forehead,
sharing tears with all Christians.
So did they take a final look at the city,
a final look at the great buildings
now consumed in flames.
They looked to the churches where the great holy edifices
were left to the merciless pagans,
the old weeping priests killed in the defense of these relics.
They looked to the seawall on the Horn,
where the Cretan soldiers in their tower
refused to surrender.
They looked to St. Sophia,

where the service of matins
was brutally ended,
the White Turbans hacking down the Imperial Gate
to slaughter and enslave the congregation.
The avenging angel never descended.
His wings remained furled;
his sword remained sheathed.[76]
And then they plunged, the Christian lords,
deep into the heart of the Turks.

What Becomes of Us

Death before the Mesoteichion.
Death by the side of kin.
Death in the name of all that one lived for.
Death before the eyes of God,
who destined such a glorious departing.
Who then can sing of such glory?
Constantine, who wished his own death?
The bards, what tale they do weave of the emperor,
who did such devastation
in the ranks of the heathens,
his Christian brethren around him,
before they were lost beneath such struggle!
Such fear that did wreck the heart of Mehmet,
when he saw the eyes of Constantine,
who no longer feared death!
A light shining through the clouds,
parting them in heavenly light,
giving the Christians a last breath!
But what truth is there in such a bard's tale?

For in that hour, that horrid hour,
when the heathens stormed the city of God,
the greatest man beneath Him,
the great Constantine,
did not embrace the fate promised him by
His Lord Jesus Christ.
He did not use his last breath in a fury
that broke shields and clove mail,
the way God had told him in these last moments.
For the city had fallen,
and righteousness no longer reigned.
God had abandoned Constantine,
had abandoned Christendom,
had let collapse all that the emperors had created
in His name.
How can one forgive such a horrid deed?
Now the emperor sought revenge on God
and did not obey His final commandment.
He did not fall beneath the Mesoteichion
and did not die where God destined him to die.
Constantine in turn betrayed God
and fled.
Fled from the city, fled from the heathens,
fled from the Christians,
fled from God.
Deep into the hills of Chios he hid,
in shame, in disgust, in such mourning
at the deed he had done.[77]
For how could he have obeyed God after the
decision the Lord had made?
But no longer could he be the strong-armed Constantine,
a name which wields His support,
a name which was crafted in His image.
No longer could he be the great Emperor of the Romans,
who, like the image of Justinian,

ruled with the cross-crested globe of God.

For like the crumbling walls of Theodosian,

a crumbling faith ensued

in Constantine's heart.

And so he became known as Yfantes,[78] and such a tale he did weave.

A song of such righteousness,

a song of the Roman's struggle against the heathens,

a song of mourning,

a song of God's betrayal.

Such is his song.

Such is my song,

for once I was known by the name Constantine,

and once I surveyed proud lands

from the steps of the now burned Hippodrome,

But God has made me what I am now,

a humble weaver,

but not of tapestries, not of cloth.

Hwaet! Listen to that which has been said

of a betrayal by the highest order,

and let it last,

so that all may learn of such treachery:

that of God, who in the hour of judgment,

left the Romans to an awful fate.

And now what becomes of us

in this godless world?

Final Historical Note

The Sultan Mehmet had promised his men a three-day sack of the city, and upon breaching the walls, the sacking commenced. Such devastation wrecked the city as the Ottomans pillaged churches, killed priests, and raped and ravaged the populace. The remaining defenders were slaughtered mercilessly, and the women were taken prisoner. Houses were ransacked and occupied by bands of armed Turks who sought all the wealth they could muster. And even though most of the city's wealth had been stripped away after the Crusader's sack of Constantinople in 1204, the Turks found their sources of wealth in the Byzantine property and in the populace itself. They tore down Justinian's statue and raided St. Sophia, where many citizens continued to pray. There they melted down the precious metals at the altars and killed the surviving clergy. Thirty thousand citizens were sold into slavery.

Mehmet grieved at the sight of the beautiful city burning and attempted to preserve some of its remaining beauty. He did so by claiming some of the most important buildings for himself and converting St. Sophia into a mosque so that it would not be burned to the ground, a fate which many of the other churches suffered. He also retained many of the existing dignitaries, such as Loukas Notaras, who continued to govern under the sultan as prefect.

The Venetian nobles were either executed or ransomed back to Italy. The Catalan consul was executed, as were other key spiritual and political figures of the Byzantines and Italians. Two of the Bocchiardo brothers survived the battle and fled the city, as did Giustiniani and four hundred others in Venetian and Genoese ships.

The Genoese colony of Pera, or Galata, had its fortifications destroyed by the Turks, and surviving Byzantine nobles who had fled to the colony were taken hostage. Mehmet felt the colony had done everything in its power to defy the Turks, and so he made sure the colony no longer wielded any authority.

The Cretan contingent in command of a sea tower never laid down their arms and continued to put up a fight. The Turks were unable to breach this tower. Eventually the sultan allowed the Cretans to return home peacefully, and they did so heroically bringing with them the tale of the city's fall.

George Sphrantzes was able to escape to Archea, where Constantine's brother Thomas ruled. George's family, however, was enslaved. Toward the end of his life, he wrote his chronicle on the family of Palaeologus and of the fall of the city. Later, he retired to a monastery in Corfu.

No evidence suggests Constantine's flight from the city. Because he took off his imperial emblem before entering the battle, his body was never identified. It is said he simply "disappeared" in the last stand of the Christians. The fate of the rest of the Palaeologus family is riddled with the deaths of its key members. Demetrios, however, deserted to the Turks, where he lived in relative comfort as a prisoner of the sultan.

It would not be long until news of the fallen city reached the ears of Europe. News of the Ottoman's power deeply distressed the people of Europe, who had not done much to avoid the fate of the Byzantines. The Turks would soon confront the Europeans, who had underestimated the power of such adversaries and had done little to stop the first great threat they posed on Christendom: the sack of Constantinople. Conflict would ensue in the following century between the Turks and the West, culminating in the Siege of Vienna in 1529, the Siege of Malta in 1565, and the Battle of Lepanto in 1571. The Ottoman Empire forged under Mehmet II lasted until the First World War.

This manuscript incorporates knowledge of ancient and medieval texts in the portrayal of the siege of Constantinople. Besides using the influence of key texts such as Homer's Iliad, the Song of Roland, Gerusalemme Liberata, and the Poetic Edda in the formation of his epic, the very words of various chronicles themselves have been used in the construction of some of the dialogues. These chronicles include the accounts written by Nester-Iskander, George Sphrantzes, Photius, Doukas, Kritovoulos, and aspects of the Law of Fratricide and the Qur'an.

Suggested Reading List

Works Cited and other Primary Sources

Barbaro, Nicolo, Giornale dell' Assedio di Constantinopoli, trans. John Melville-Jones, 1969.

Beg, Tursun, History of Mehmet the Conqueror, as documented in Pertusi, Angelo, La Caduta di Constantinopoli, vol. 1, pp. 304–331, 1976.

Doukas, Fragmenta Historicum Graecorum, vol. 5, Paris, 1870.

Homer. The Iliad, trans. Richmond Lattimore, 1961.

'Kanunname' as the Law of Fratricide, as documented in Uzunçarsılı, . H., Anadolu Beylikleri, 1937.

Kritovoulos, Critobuli Imbriotae Historiae, Diether Reinsch, 1983.

Nestor-Iskander, The Tale of Constantinople, trans. and ed. Walter K. Hanak and Marios Philippides, 1998.

Photius, Homilies, trans. Cyril Alexander Mango, 1958.

Robert of Clari, The Conquest of Constantinople, trans. E.H. McNeal, 1996.

Sphrantzes, George, The Fall of the Byzantine Empire: A Chronicle by George Sphantzes 1401–1477, trans. Marios Philippides, 1980.

The Poetic Edda, trans. Carolyne Larrington, 1996.

The Song of Roland, trans. Glyn Burgess, 1990.

Tasso, Torquato, Gerusalemme Liberata, trans. J.H. Wiffen, 2007.

Qur'an, trans. M.A.S. Abdel Haleem, 2008.

Secondary Sources

Akbar, M. J., The Shade of Swords: Jihad and the Conflict Between Islam and Christianity, London, 2002.

Alderson, A. D., The Structure of the Ottoman Dynasty, Oxford, 1956.

Babinger, Franz, Mehmet the Conqueror and His Time, trans. Ralph Manheim, Princeton, 1978.

Crowley, Roger, Constantinople, the Last Great Siege 1453, London, 2005.

Kinross, Lord, The Ottoman Centuries, London, 1977.

Norwich, John J., A History of Byzantium, London, 1995.

Pertusi, Angelo, La Caduta di Constantinopoli, vol. 1, 1976.

Tsangadas, Bryon, The Fortifications and Defense of Constantinople, New York, 1980.

Notes

1. Old English for "Listen."

2. Traditionally, and in the form of the Iliad, Homer invokes the Muses. In this case, in a Christian context, the Muses are replaced by Jesus and the Saints.

3. The wall that surrounded Constantinople, originally built by Emperor Theodosian II in AD 408, completed in AD 413. Under the direction of a Praetorian prefect Anthemius, the wall stretched 6.5 kilometers from the Marmara Sea to the Golden Horn, enclosing the city. The wall was considered impregnable, holding against the fiercest sieges from Avars, Arabs, Bulgars, and Rus. Only twice was it ever breached: in 1204 by the Crusaders of the Fourth Crusade, and in 1453 by the Ottoman Turks.

4. Byzantines called themselves "Romans," still considering themselves a part of the empire which had fallen in the west. The term "Byzantine" did not come about in the English language until 1853.

5. Introduction format adapted from that of Homer's Iliad. Starting from the invoking of the Muses, the protagonist of Constantine and the antagonist of Mehmet emerge.

6. Paraphrase from the Qur'an, Surah Aal 'Imran, 3:64.

7. The Byzantine Emperor Heraclius ascended the throne of Byzantium through a rebellion against the previous emperor Phocas. This internal rebellion had stripped the troops from the frontier of the Empire and led to outside pressure from the Persian Sassanids to the east and Avars to the west. The initial campaign against these external enemies was disastrous, and military defeat after military defeat followed. The Persians continued to annex more territory of Byzantium until Heraclius devised a way to reorder the military of the empire. Using an innovative system consisting of the granting of land to those who would give the emperor military service, he succeeded in taking back lands captured by hostile neighbors. In his campaign, he succeeded in restoring the Church of the Holy Sepulchre in Jerusalem and subsequently the True Cross, which had been taken by the Persians and Hebrews in 614.

8. Sons of Orhan: Ottoman Turks. The origins of the Ottoman Turks is shrouded in myth, but that which has been confirmed tells of a small band of illiterate warriors, Turkmen, who lived a nomadic lifestyle among horses, tents, and open fires, and who around 1208 began to band together. It is said that Osman, the father of Orhan, dreamed of a strong empire equal to that of Byzantium, which he looked upon from the steppes with longing and envy. In a dream Osman saw Constantinople as the center point of the world, the "diamond mounted between two sapphires and two emeralds, and appeared thus to form the precious stone of the ring of a vast dominion which embraced the entire world" (Kinross, p. 24). From that day forth, it became the destiny of the offspring of the Osman family to conquer that part of the world.

9. This is a reference to War Elephants used by Persians at the Battle of Guagamela in 331 BC and at the Battle of Avarayr in AD 451.

10. Paraphrase from Qu'ran, Surah 30, Al-Room.

11. Greek fire, the exact components of which are still unknown, was used against this Arab invasion. This petroleum based mixture would have to be put out using sand or dirt. It was used in the form of incendiary arrows, firepots, and was discharged through tubes. Mounted on the prow of a ship, Greek fire could be especially devastating to other vessels at sea.

12. Name referring to all peoples of Western Europe by the Byzantines. In this case, it refers to the Crusaders of the Fourth Crusade. In 1204 they sacked the city, for wealth needed to wage their crusade. The Crusaders, who initially wanted to invade the Muslim East through Egypt and then capture Jerusalem, looked to the Venetians for transport across the seas. Venice agreed to transport around 33,500 Crusaders to Egypt. The Crusaders arrived at the city, but much fewer than were expected, and thus were unable to pay the 85,000 silver marks that the Venetians requested for their services. The Doge used this opportunity to have the Crusaders do Venetian dirty work in order to pay the debt. This involved the sacking of Zara, and finally the sack of Constantinople. A three day sack of the city by the Crusaders stripped the Byzantines of most objects of Greek and Roman antiquity which had been contained in the city, an event which is seen as the beginning of the decline of the Byzantine Empire, for they never fully recovered from such a devastating blow.

13. Saint Sophia was the Orthodox cathedral built in only six years by Emperor Justinian in 537. Its immense beauty and numerous relics of various saints and Jesus Christ made it the center of the Christian world. It contained intensely colored mosaics of icons and saints and gold-plated walls. Its beauty was so extraordinary that when Russian travelers came back from Constantinople after visiting the cathedral and the lavish, gorgeous rituals contained within, they brought orthodoxy back to Russia. It was in Saint Sophia that the Russian states officially converted to orthodoxy. Besides religion, Russia incorporated the written language of the Byzantines, the Cyrillic alphabet,

for their own uses. Saint Sophia, with the sack by the Turks, had its walls stripped of their value, and many mosaics were destroyed for their iconography (which is shunned by Muslims) and were then replaced by Arabic calligraphy. Mehmet did realize the great beauty of the place, and instead of destroying it completely, he built minarets and converted it to a mosque. It is now known as Hagia Sophia.

14. Paraphrase of Paul the Silentiary, officer of Justinian I, see Norwich, vol. I, p. 202.

15. In 1451, Sultan Murat, the predecessor to Mehmet, left behind a son Ahmet when the he died. Mehmet, in order to secure the throne, dispatched a lackey to the quarters of Murat's wife, who was grieving at Mehmet's court. The lackey, by the name Ali Bey, drowned Ahmet in his bath. The next day, Mehmet fixed the crime on Ali Bey, who was executed, and married Ahmet's mother, Murat's wife, to a noble. Ahmet and his mother were the only ones who opposed Mehmet's ascendance, hence when they were dispatched of, Mehmet was considered the rightful ruler. It was then that he moved the capital to Edirne. The people of Constantinople knew of this episode in Ottoman history, but did not act on any insights into Mehmet's murderous character.

16. George Sphranzes is paralleled to the classical figure of Odysseus by being described in the form of Odysseus from the Iliad, p. 83, 105. Both figures were great wise men of council, both as lordly, if not more lordly then those they worked for. In Odysseus's case, this is Achilles and Agamemnon, and in George's case, it is Constantine XI. George was also a very close friend of the emperor. Odysseus may have held the same amount of respect for his lord.

17. By the middle of the fifteenth century, Ottoman dominance was clear. The small bit of territory the Byzantine Emperor retained was almost powerless, nestled in the middle of the Turkish Empire which reached from Anatolia to Hungary. Edirne was the powerful capital of the Ottoman Empire, and it lay on the European side of the empire. When Mehmet set forth on his

campaign, it was from Edirne that the majority of the Muslim armies gathered and marched toward Constantinople.

18. Paraphrase from Kanunname as the Law of Fratricide in Uzunçarsılı, p. 45. Fratricide was not uncommon at the Ottoman court, but was exercised by sultans with the overlying belief that an empire should remain undivided and under one supreme ruler. Mehmet II legally sanctioned fratricide in his Kanunname, drawing support from passages of the Qur'an.

19. The word Saracen had been used before 1095, the year of the First Crusade, as a derogatory name for Muslims. After the fall of Constantinople however in 1453, the word Saracen was replaced by Turk, which became the new derogatory name for Muslims. The Turks would refer to themselves as Ottoman, or Seljuk, depending on their origins, never referring to themselves as Turks. This word became embedded in the English language and is now considered acceptable and not necessarily derogatory.

20. Once again, God is placed in the position of the Muses, as the determiner of fate. Here too is a reference that brings together pagan Norse belief and Christian faith. As in the Norse Poetic Edda, the three fates beneath the tree called Yggdrasill weave the fate of men. They are called Fated, Becoming, and Must-Be, and they come "knowing a great deal" (p. 6) to carve upon wooden ships and determine the fate of all.

21. Paraphrase from The Poetic Edda, p. 6.

22. George Sphranztes holds as much in common with Odysseus as he does with Nestor of Pylos. Here George Sphrantzes emulates Nestor, as he speaks of a golden era in Byzantine history, before the arrival of the Crusaders in 1204. Nestor, despite ranking below people such as Achilles and Agamemnon, was so wise and knowledgeable that he commanded immense respect and was always heeded. Like Agamemnon and Achilles, Constantine, although emperor, looks up to George, who is as wise as Nestor.

23. A description attributed to the Song of Roland. In this poem about Charlemagne and his conquests in Spain against the

pagan Marsile, the author constantly describes the Emperor Charlemagne as a man of immense wisdom. In order to characterize this learnedness, he uses phrases such as his "hoary-white beard" as to embody such wisdom. A white beard would be the mark of one who has undergone much and is the just ruler, one both wise and knowledgeable.

24. This humanization of God is used in Torquato Tasso's Gerusalemme Liberata, which was in turn used from the influence of the Iliad. Throughout the Iliad, the gods are portrayed in human form, have a direct relation and influence on the people of the world, and sometimes even heed the calls of the mortals. The humanization of God in the same way as in the Iliad can be slightly dangerous in a medieval text, as it may undermine God's mighty image by giving him human characteristics and human emotion. By showing the human emotion in God, however, a more Renaissance spiritual connection between the faithful and God might emerge, God becoming a less feared and more connected image to the secular world. Tasso was commissioned by the Pope to write his epic, and perhaps the Pope viewed this humanization as a way to show God's renewed, personal connection with people.

25. In Torquato Tasso's Gerusalemme Liberata, Gabriel is dispatched as a messenger from God to speak to the Crusaders Godfrey and Baldwin. The angel comes in his own form, not afraid to show himself as a divine being in front of a mortal. In the Iliad, however, when the gods intervene, they always take the form of a mortal, and in the mortal's image, inspire with godly words and actions. In the case of Gabriel's mission to deliver a message to Constantine, the more classical form is used, as the angel takes the form of a watchman, who without the aid of God, would not have seen the construction of Rumeli Hisari that was to follow.

26. The colony of Pera, or Galata, was a port of Genoa that lay to the North of the Golden Horn and Constantinople. The port felt the same threat as Constantinople did with the building of the Rumeli Hisari. In order to cope with this threat they chose

to not confront Mehmet and jeopardize their trade opportunities, but instead made arrangements should Constantinople fall. Sympathies for fellow Christians across the Horn, however, remained, and the Genoese would not be reluctant to secretly aid their brothers to the south.

27. The Rumeli Hisari, which can be translated as "Throat Cutter," was a fortress built by Mehmet on the European side of the Bosphorus just north of Galata. Mehmet and his predecessor had spent years ferrying Turks to and fro, being that the Ottoman Empire stretched on both sides of the Bosphorus. The Dardanelles were blocked by Latin merchants, however, and the route to the Black Sea was blocked by Byzantine ships. Because of this, Mehmet saw the control of the Bosphorus essential to unifying the Ottoman Empire and in ending Constantinople's supremacy it had gained because of its great trade location. During the siege to follow, the control of the Bosphorus by the Rumeli Hisari would make the food supply from Latin and Byzantine colonies on the Black Sea unable to reach the city. In order to assure Ottoman supremacy, the Rumeli Hisari was garrisoned by 400 troops and armed with large cannons, which could send 600 pound stone balls into the hulls of passing ships.

28. As in the case of the chronicler Doukas, people from the West, especially the Italians, were referred to as Latins.

29. Paraphrase from Doukas, Fragmenta, p. 239.

30. Throughout the Middle Ages, God was seen as the one to decide victory in battle. Although military might and strategy did play a large part in combat, it was essentially left to God to decide the outcome, and the winner of the battle would be considered God's favorite contender.

31. Paraphrase from Doukas, Fragmenta, p. 245.

32. Paraphrase from Tursun Beg, History of Mehmet the Conqueror, as documented in La Caduta, p. 311. The dragons were cannons mounted on the walls of the Rumeli Hisari so that boats traveling through the Bosphorus either two or from

the Black Sea would have to submit first to the Turks who demanded a tax and searched the vessel. These cannons were as large as twenty-seven feet long with a diameter of thirty inches and were able to send stones weighing up to 600 pounds into the hulls of ships that refused to stop at the Rumeli Hisari.

33. Eye-witness accounts, like that by Jacopo de Campi, graphically describe this punishment.

34. Constantine XI sent pleas to the Venetians, the Genoese, the Pope, Hungary, Aragon and Naples, and Dubrovnik. The Venetians and Genoese did not want to jeopardize their trade with the Ottomans now that they realized the Byzantine Empire was falling, and so sent very empty responses to Constantine. The Genoese, fearing for their colonies of Chios and Galata, had their senate make the best possible agreements with Mehmet should the city fall. Pope Nicholas was still reluctant to send aid to Orthodox Christians, after events such as the Schism tore the Churches apart, but he did manage to convince the Holy Roman Emperor, Frederick III, to send an ultimatum to Mehmet, which had little affect. Alfonso of Aragon and Naples did dispatch a flotilla to sail to Constantinople, but it was soon after retracted.

35. The Great Schism of 1054 left Christianity split between Catholicism and orthodoxy. On the 16th day of July that year, Humbert of Mourmoutiers placed a bill of excommunication of the altar of St. Sophia. Rome had sent Humbert to settle the disputes between the Church of Rome and the Byzantine Church. Since then, the two Churches remained rivals and were ever reluctant to aid the other in times of need.

36. The Morea was the name given to the Byzantine controlled area of the Peloponnese. Here Constantine's brothers Thomas and Demetrios lay besieged by troops sent by Mehmet, so that they could not send aid to their brother to the north.

37. John of Germany was actually a Scotsman, an engineer who was extremely skillful in less orthodox ways of combat. His knowledge of mining would be invaluable in the events to come.

38. Paraphrase from Sphrantzes, p. 72.

39. Provinces and important cities of the Ottoman Empire. Turks from all corners of the empire came with great speed to Mehmets call, and the thought of conquest brought not only soldiers to the cause, but numerous bands of thieves and criminals made their way to Mehmet's side. The speed at which Mehmet mustered his troops still startles historians.

40. The exact amount of troops of both Mehmet and Constantine's armies is still speculative as the many accounts of the battle include extreme exaggeration and fictionalization. In reality, the Muslim army was approximately 200,000 strong, and Constantine commanded a combined 8,000 men. The Muslim army was made up of siphas, or provincial cavalry, azaps, or Christian conscript peasants, and Janissaries, paid professional soldiers who made up the strongest section of the army. Janissaries were greatly feared by the Christians, being that they were made up of mostly Christian Slavs who were abducted at a young age by the sultan and were brought up to be the most radical and best trained soldiers. Constantine's army was somewhat divided being that it included people from Italy, Spain, the Greek islands, and the surrounding Byzantine area. This would be a major factor in the battle for the city as people from different regions would find it difficult to cooperate.

41. The Imperial Palace of the emperors. This area of the wall was targeted by the Turks as one of the weaker sections, as the palace protruded slightly when constructed, and a new wall had to be built to surround it. This separate section of the wall was not as thick or tall as its counterpart constructed by Theodosian.

42. Reference to Achilles, who throughout the Iliad is described as swift-footed. Both he and Giustiniani were greatest among men when it came to the workings of war.

43. This area of the wall was considered the weakest part, and as the central section, would be where the heart of the battle took place. The weakness of the wall was partly because of a drainage stream that flowed from the city and into the Lycus valley, located in the central region of the land outside the wall. This valley sloped

downward slightly which allowed the Mehmet, stationed on a hill, to look downward on the city, over the first wall. This section was also one of the oldest parts of the wall, and was crumbling before Giustiniani made his repairs. Because of the weakness the Mesoteichion posed, the strongest Christian troops were stationed there: Giustiniani and his well-armed Genoese men-at-arms as well as the personal troop of Constantine.

44. Paraphrase from Nestor-Iskander, p. 35.

45. The dragons here once again refer to the Great Cannons, which Mehmet fired on the walls. At first the physical effect was not evident, but the psychological effects cast the populace into a temporary panic. Cannons were extremely rare, and not many had ever laid eyes, let alone laid ears, on such a devastating weapon. The cannons were the result of the changing style of warfare, and at the time of the siege the Byzantines, although they had a few cannons of their own (albeit not close to the huge scale of the Turkish cannons), were living in the old ways. The cannons versus the wall became essentially a struggle between old and new.

46. Reference to Constantine I, founder of Constantinople. Born in AD 272, Constantine was the first to legalize Christianity in the Roman Empire, and although he spent his entire life as a pagan, he converted on his deathbed in 337.

47. The walls had been breached in fact, once before, by the Franks in 1204. The cannons, however, dealt an unparalleled amount of damage in a surprisingly short time, something the Franks were not able to accomplish with their more medieval siege devices.

48. Recall the Janissaries who wore white turbans. The rest of the Muslim army was dressed with red turbans; the red turbans were a symbol of the ordinary stature of the troops.

49. Word for a shirt of chain mail from Old English.

50. Although this is a very Iliad-like moment, the fate of a battle being decided by the two commanders of the opposing armies, the way the fight is described resembles the form used frequently in the Song of Roland. It was quite improbable that

two commanders would engage in such a duel as their two armies looked on in this age of warfare. The duel is a throwback to the bygone era of Homer and the Greeks, when such events could have possibly occurred.

51. He was the commander of the fleet, which held about 140 vessels. It was made up of twelve to eighteen large war galleys, seventy to eighty smaller fustae, and twenty-five transport vessels. The fleet set out from the Dardanelles and on April 2 arrived at the chain, where the Byzantine fleet assembled. It was hardly a Byzantine fleet, however, instead being composed of ships from Genoa, Ancona, Crete, Spain, Venice, and Provence.

52. Manuel II, father of Constantine XI.

53. Paraphrase from Doukas, Fragmenta, p. 269.

54. The details of this event are still unknown, but on the 22 of April, the Ottoman fleet which had so far been unsuccessful, finally presented a formidable force to the Christians. Entry into the Golden Horn was seen by the Turks as the first step toward victory. By pressing both the land and seawalls, the already stretched defenders would have to further stretch themselves as to protect both walls. The chain which protected the Golden Horn had, since the seventh century AD, been able to successfully keep out invaders, and only Mehmet's ingenuity allowed the Turks to bypass it. Mehmet put into effect a successful plan, which, using a system of logs and pulleys, allowed the transportation of the entire Turkish fleet from the Bosphorus, around Pera, across the land, and finally into the Horn. The defenders at the time would have looked on with horror as the land-bound fleet seemed like a mythological occurrence, a deed only the divine could accomplish. Much of Mehmet's ingenuity was made a reality as a result of the immense manpower at his fingertips.

55. The Latin States refers to present day Italy.

56. Realistically, the number of Italian soldiers who were impaled after their defeat in the Horn was around forty, Giacomo Coco included. Mehmet had fought and schemed with deliberate

psychological warfare, to great effect, and the impaling of these Italian soldiers in clear view of the walls of Constantinople was just another way to strike fear into the hearts of the defenders.

57. Matthew 5:39.

58. In the medieval period, a common approach to natural disasters or defeat in war was God's punishment for the sins committed by the people. The Viking ravages against Britain in the eighth and ninth centuries beginning with the sack of Lindisfarne in 793, for example, was seen by British monks as divine retribution.

59. This description of siege ladders stretching from the ships is attributed to Robert of Clari, The Conquest of Constantinople, pp. 70–71. A knight who participated on the Fourth Crusade, Robert witnessed the assault by the crusaders on the walls of Constantinople in 1204. This ingenious siege equipment was devised by the Venetian Doge and used to great effect, and much to the dismay of the Byzantines. It is possible Mehmet may have used similar tactics.

60. Paraphrase from Nestor-Iskander, p. 43.

61. Paraphrase from Nestor-Iskander, p. 45.

62. Another moment from the Iliad. Once again it is up to the divine to determine the outcome of battles, and although Man may do all in their power to forge their own fate, in the end it is up to the gods to shine pity on them or leave them to the workings of the world. The duel between these two lords actually did take place, and chroniclers do speak about the brave Greek soldier who saved Giustiniani by cutting off Murat's leg. In this case it is Gabriel who, in the form of the Greek soldier, saves Giustiniani.

63. Mehmet continued to display his genius after he took the Horn. He constructed towers exceeding the height of the walls, filled them with men, and attempted to take the battlements. Eyewitness accounts tell of covered causeways of wood and skins that provided the attackers constant cover from the missiles cast from the walls. Being that such towers were exceedingly difficult to take along the long march from Edirne, Mehmet

created these towers during the siege, assembling them on site using stores of lumber cut down from the surrounding area. These towers were extremely effective psychologically, being that they were rare objects remembered only in stories of battles long past. They temporarily sent the defenders into a panic, before a way to destroy them was devised. The defenders did so by rolling barrels of gunpowder from the walls.

64. Whilst in combat, Mehmet employed brutal men with whips called *chavushes*. This was used to ensure that any fleeing soldiers would think twice about leaving the battlefield.

65. Mining warfare was an extremely difficult aspect of medieval siege warfare, but extremely effective. Stout walls of countless castles had proved too strong for ordinary siege weapons (until the arrival of the cannon), and mining was seen as a great option for entrance to the castle. Either the attackers would make their way completely under the walls and emerge on the other side, or the attackers would place timber and pitch at the foundation of the wall and set it alight, collapsing the wall from below. The mine warfare occurring at Constantinople was extremely complex, involving numerous tunnels mined by Saxon conscripts for Mehmet's purpose. John of Germany would then construct counter-tunnels which would find their way into the tunnels of the intruders, where the men would do battle and attempt to collapse each other's tunnel. Candlelit battles in an environment where oxygen was sparse and constant threat of collapse plagued the men would have been quite fearsome and terrible.

66. The Hodegetria was an icon of the Virgin Mary holding Jesus Christ, and was believed by the Byzantines to be invested with many supernatural abilities. It was said to have been painted by St. Luke the Evangelist, and had been paraded on the ramparts of Constantinople during the countless sieges of the city including the siege of the Avars in AD 626 the siege of the Arabs in AD 718. The victories during these sieges were attributed to the Hodegetria's powers.

67. Quoted from Photius, Homily III and IV.

68. As witnessed by Kritovoulos, Critobuli, p. 58.

69. The light of St. Sophia was supposedly granted by God to Justinian in preservation of Christianity and in the upholding of the faith. When this light left the city it was seen, along with the other mysterious events, as the will of God to hand the city over to the Turks—the ultimate departure of God from the city. The white mist, the red fog, the fleeing light, and the storm all actually happened, and are attributed to volcanic activity. In around 1453, on the island of Kuwae in the Pacific, a volcano exploded, destroying the island itself. With a force two million times the atomic bomb of Hiroshima, rock and dust was blasted into the atmosphere. Being sulfur rich, the soil of Kuwae, which now flowed throughout the atmosphere, changed the climate drastically as it was pushed west. This cloud of dust brought snow to areas known for warmth and destroyed countless harvests on its way toward Constantinople. It was the volcanic particles that in 1453 found themselves overlooking the siege, and it is this volcanic activity paired with discharges of atmospheric electricity that caused the light of God and the other strange events. In a world devoid of such science, however, these occurrences would have been seen as portents, and they would have been interpreted as signs from God signifying, in this case, the fall of the city. The Turks also had interpreted these omens, embracing them as they promised victory.

70. The Varangian Guard was a loyal band of mercenaries, originally recruited from Scandinavia by Emperor Basil II in order to eliminate the Byzantine royal guard, whose loyalties often shifted, leading to great upheaval. In the later centuries, the Guard was mostly composed of people from the British Isles. Although there is little evidence of their presence during the siege of 1453, Varangians have been identified in Constantinople as late as 1400.

71. The final conflict at the walls of Constantinople was essentially delivered in four phases. The first phase was the largest bombardment in the history of Medieval Europe: an attempt to destroy the remainder of the wall Giustiniani constructed, and

strike fear in the hearts of the defenders. The second stage was the wave of azaps, the common soldiers, to dull the defenders and weaken them physically and mentally. The third wave was of the Anatolian heavy infantry, and the fourth wave, led by Mehmet himself, consisted of the heavily armored shock troops of the Muslim army: the white turban Janissaries. This was the final attempt to break the defenders and storm the city.

72. The eclipse is not fictional. After the many omens represented by the events occurring because of the eruption on the island of Kuwae, the defenders were devastated psychologically. After over fifty days of siege, horrible conditions, constant bombardment, and no sight of a relief force, the defenders clung desperately to a nonexistent hope. The lunar eclipse was possibly the final event which completely turned the tide of the war. The moon passing over the sun created the image of the crescent moon, which was the symbol of the Turks. Looking upon the Turkish emblem in the sky, the defenders must have been stricken with incredible fear, and the attackers must have been greatly inspired.

73. This moment in history is worthy of Homer. It is a complete and sudden reversal of fortune in the midst of the battle, as if the gods themselves intervened. The hero of the story is all of a sudden struck down in a quite unlikely way, and a misunderstanding causes the flight of the Italians. The defenders, who so nearly found themselves at the altar of victory, now face the worst possible consequences, and it is no longer in the hands of people like Constantine or Giustiniani to alter their fate.

74. The Bocchiardo brothers had successfully defended the Blachernae palace part of the wall. Through a series of posterns, they, with a small band of their heavily armored men, made numerous sallies from the walls, catching the Turks by surprise. On one of their sallies, upon returning from a successful raid, one soldier forgot to close the sally port behind him. The Turks discovered this unlocked door and burst through, catching the Italians by surprise. Although the Turks were eventually furiously repelled by the Bocchiardo brothers, the Turks had managed to pull down the Palaeologus flag, and lift the sultan's flag

in its place. To the south at the Mesoteichion, the defenders wedged between the walls thought the city had been breached, and faltered again in the face of the Turks.

75. The same reference as the "Son's of Orhan." In this case Constantine is referring to Orhan's father Osman.

76. This is a reference to the prophecy that should an enemy enter the city as far as the Column of Constantine, which was near Saint Sophia, an angel would descend to defend the populace.

77. Evidence and eyewitness accounts point to Constantine dying in the last stand against the Ottomans. His body was never identified, however, as he pulled off his imperial insignia so that the Turks could not desecrate his body once he was identified as the emperor. He is said to have simply "disappeared" in the final struggle. Because of the lack of concrete evidence explaining the fate of Constantine, here he does not die but flees the city in shame and defeat.

78. A Byzantine name of the early fourteenth century derived from the trade of a weaver.

listen|imagine|view|experience

AUDIO BOOK DOWNLOAD INCLUDED WITH THIS BOOK!

In your hands you hold a complete digital entertainment package. In addition to the paper version, you receive a free download of the audio version of this book. Simply use the code listed below when visiting our website. Once downloaded to your computer, you can listen to the book through your computer's speakers, burn it to an audio CD or save the file to your portable music device (such as Apple's popular iPod) and listen on the go!

How to get your free audio book digital download:

1. Visit www.tatepublishing.com and click on the elLIVE logo on the home page.
2. Enter the following coupon code:
    f0ec-6172-5b0a-1be1-bb75-320a-e6ef-7f11
3. Download the audio book from your elLIVE digital locker and begin enjoying your new digital entertainment package today!